UNBOUND

UNBOUND

A BOOK OF AIDS

Aaron Shurin

NIGHTBOAT BOOKS
NEW YORK

ISBN: 978-1-64362-154-8

An earlier version of *Unbound: A Book of AIDS* was published by Sun and Moon Press in 1997.

Cover image: © J. John Priola
Design and typesetting by adam b. bohannon
Typeset in Bodoni

Cataloging-in-publication data is available from the Library of Congress

Nightboat Books
New York
www.nightboat.org

A NOTE ON THE TEXT

The pieces in *Unbound: A Book of AIDS* came together from various trajectories: as essays, poetics, solo talks, conference presentations, literary criticism, dance-texts, and poems. It was as if every valence in life were commandeered by the virus, so that one needed every form of literary address to meet it. This expanded Nightboat edition marks twenty-five years since the original publication by Sun & Moon Press in 1997; a selection then appeared as part of my essay collection, *The Skin of Meaning*, in 2016. Consequently, there are three introductions to the work, each trying to catch the overflow of meanings of the epidemic from a slightly different angle; each trying to draw a connective arc across the range of sorrowful and beatific revelations.

The tenor was always one of unfolding incredulity, and the ground a portion of history held in a desperate embrace. The book opens, now, with a new preface, "Rebinding *Unbound*," while the two earlier introductions form an Epilogue: the anthology preface first, followed by the original 1997 version. *Unbound*, then, ends where it began, with sorrow, wonder, memory, history and hope uncharted, open to the wind.

CONTENTS

Rebinding *Unbound*
A Re-introduction to *Unbound: A Book of AIDS*

The bristles rising on the back of your neck, a sense of silent footsteps behind you closing in, the bewildering proliferation of medical terminology, a matrix of conjectural timelines and invisible transmissions: As the COVID-19 pandemic rages around us, building its houses of terror, how could I not recall that other epidemic, unrelenting, ferocious, which wiped out much of my extended (gay) family (among 700,000 other U. S. Americans of every race and several sexual persuasions)—all of them extinguished by the relentless acronym: AIDS.

My book of essays, poems, and assorted texts, revived here—*Unbound: A Book of AIDS*—was originally published in 1997, though the writing had begun a decade earlier. Even then life in San Francisco was well-saturated and transformed by the mysterious viral complex. I, too, was saturated and transformed—by loss, by grief, by constant terror, but also by friends who rose to the occasion of their dying newly empowered, with sudden wisdom and unsentimental clarity. Both the horrors and the graces were overwhelming, the more so because I'd begun to feel something like responsibility—to scale the walls surrounding the LGBTQ (especially the G) communities, and raise the alarm to inform the blindfolded citizens that a cataclysmic illness was being visited upon their (especially) fathers, brothers, and sons. It was as if we were living in an actual walled city—community as quarantine?—and no one on the outside could even conceive of the misery or dignity taking place within. Within, the drama was unrelenting, conflicted; even now I can feel the tense unknowingness, the ball and chain attached to test results, the quiet violence of waiting, the agony of joy. It was as if we were living in an opera, except the high-vaulting arias were our everyday talk, and the wrenching love duets our nightly bedside visits with Robert or Jim.

*

I wasn't (as I originally noted) an authority—neither a scientist nor a sociologist—but I was/I am a poet, perpetually in search of meaning. I let my friends lead me through the thicket of multiplying symptoms, false cures, and assorted revelations. I found that writing about my friends brought our companionship into greater focus, an ancillary treasure to the duty of bearing witness. Decoding speech and analyzing actions—the care embedded in writing, in paying scrupulous attention—laid bare the common bonds, and open hearts, of friendship. The real geniuses among the infected invited their friends in to the zone of approaching death so they might share not the darkness but the awakenings, and return, enlarged, to their previously normal lives.

The corona pandemic! How could we possibly have imagined a second visitation in such a short time, wielding such a similar scythe, and equally propelled by government indifference and neglect? But the COVID-19 virus moves so fast and AIDS moved so slowly! The mark of this pandemic is how boldly the virus strikes, progressing with uncommon speed, often isolating patients at diagnosis, and instantly exiling loved ones to the outer-lands, hurtling the infected from intubation to tombstone in a matter of days. The mark of AIDS was how stealthily it struck, how it grew in a slow desperate progression, often unmaking the body in protracted stages, so that loved ones endured seeing the disfiguration, the withering away, the sleepless eyes trolling the dark. And yet *Unbound* mainly pursues the other side, where those with the virus have time to meet their mortality, to absorb the unimaginable and give shape and voice to its lessons, to rise above the falling spirit in tender dramas of salvation—or with a cognizant wink restage in full riot the comedy of errors of terrors. These things I've witnessed—humble interlocutor in awe before men of such bravery, such creativity, hilarity, willpower, insight, as to outmaneuver the fatal winds and compose their epitaphs in updrafts. Circles of farewells, organized meals by the hour or day, emergency telephone trees or email loops, and rounds of saintly visitors with large ears and soft voices: How lucky we were to be able to display our affection; how grateful to have the luxury of properly saying goodbye.

*

Twenty-five years later, in the middle of this new pandemic, *Unbound*'s urgent empathy is renewed. The AIDS-inflected stories of purple bodies and haunted places, of plotted memorials and crushing numbers, of indomitability and attitude-in-the-face-of, speak to the corona virus as from an older brother of terror to a younger, one set of grief and struggle reinforcing the other. COVID-19 calls to HIV in mortal consanguinity: two deathtraps at century's end and century's beginning, two agitators inflaming the transit zone between life and death, challenging our concepts of health, vulnerability, guilt, religiosity, solitude, security, community, isolation, and hope.

*

There's a certain naiveté to some of the writing in *Unbound,* a gloss of innocence: I knew very little about death at the outset, and very much by the end. Is grief itself developmental? I think it grew as my writing grew, found its measure in the cacophony of names and voices, the roll call of implacable fate. I think it grew as the epidemic grew, from the spectral tremors of first encounter, to the reverberations of impossible extent. I think grief took hold as the virus does, lodged deep in the tissues and fluids and blood. Twenty-five years later it resurfaces intact, comprehensive, unwavering: a background, an imminence.

*

Unbound was the instructional medium through which I attempted to integrate the decimations of AIDS; it rubbed out the sting, licked the wounds, and swallowed the venom. I turned to sentences and narrative to participate in stories that made the invisible malevolence concrete, to put it in a human context, a body, a person: *my* Jackson, *my* Johnny, *my* Chuck. HIV wasn't a grand figure, caped and marauding; it was the daily news, right in your face, grotesquely demotic. Yet as if by collective agreement there would be no common mass graves here; every perished host would be named out loud (see the Names Project, the Bay Area Reporter obits, or the AIDS memorial grove)— just as the lesbian/gay movement had transitioned from shamed silence to righteous, outspoken rebellion. I learned to act in part as a ventriloquist, through which my infected friends spoke the revelations they wanted to transmit; in part as a scribe, adhering to the malodorous facts; and in part as a writer, seizing on sentences to unknot the congeries of information and emotion, to fold Marshall or Ken into phrases of time and space, and pinch their cheeks to raise the blood and draw them back to a place among the living.

*

Unbound is arranged chronologically and carries some of the detective-like tensions that characterized the early epidemic: the elemental drama of unmasking the virus itself and naming its assault; the grand guignol theater of young men disappearing piece by piece week by week, on the street, at the café, at the gym; the tense narrative progressions of personal struggle and personal reward, of each aching trajectory from hospital to hospice to home.

I've added one final piece to the book, written several years after the others but very much a part of the compositional ethos. The Age of AIDS bleeds through running decades. This is the third introduction I've written for *Unbound*, and each iteration casts a different light on what is essentially unfathomable. Grieving, wailing, mourning, missing, weeping, suffering, sighing, crying, seeing, rising, reviving, transcending, overcoming, unbinding, unbending, unbound.

I tried to honor the lives I lost. I tried to make a zone of history quiver. I tried to hold my head above water so I could see farther. I tried to model your tender cheek and the swipe of your neck. I tried to thread idiosyncrasy and predicament and chance to make a day like a day, I tried to hold suspense and find the rhythms of actions and intents. I tried to get out of the way while I was talking, and respect each virus as an adversary, and make the shape of a life discernable—for a moment, at least. I tried to craft a eulogy for a city in time. I tried to make a space where you could unwind your memories, hang them out like linen to dry in the sun, and I hung mine out too, and the air was breathable.

"Common measure in homage to fitting company," says the poem "Human Immune."

Here is *Unbound: A Book of AIDS*:

A.S./2021

UNBOUND

Full Circle
Postscript to "City of Men"

When I read my erotic rampage, "City of Men," to a group of students a couple of years back, one aw shucks type with wider than ever eyes responded: "Boy, that sure isn't safe sex!" Chagrined, I held up the pages, pointing to the poem itself, the act of writing it. "No," I smiled, "*this* is safe sex!" But—chastened—I'd copped out; it was exactly what I had *not* intended with "City of Men."

I did have a hidden agenda. The poem uses only Whitman's language, culled from poems in the Children of Adam and Calamus groupings from *Leaves of Grass.* As most careful readers of Whitman know, "Calamus" is his collection of homoerotic love poems, emotional, tender, idealistic, radically political, prophetic, obliquely erotic, but—alas—not sexual. If you want sex, go to the grouping "Children of Adam," Whitman's putative heterosexual songs. They are filled with body and body parts, physical material catalogues, paeans to the sex act—but—alas—no love. The body is electric but it is not affectionate.

I have read Whitman's private journals, the most private parts, where they are written partially in code to keep the secret—perhaps from himself as well as others—of his love for Peter Doyle, the secret—but we've heard this many times from the 19th and 20th centuries—torment of his awakening but not yet awake homosexuality, the revelations of his self-expressed desire to (using for homoeroticism his code word "adhesiveness") "depress the adhesive nature/ It is in excess—making life a torment/ All this diseased, feverish, disproportionate *adhesiveness*." Depress it *in himself!* Anyone who has been there can immediately recognize the call of the closet. This pernicious disregard for truth caught Whitman—in spite of his revolutionary outspokenness about sex and the body as well as male/male affection—and forced him to sever his love poems—his writing of eros— into two mutually exclusive—and incomplete—halves.

My historical period has permitted me to come full circle, to write my eros out of spirit and body, shamelessly, and perhaps for the first time in history from a completely integrated viewpoint. In composing "City of Men" I chose to graft—by interspersing them—words from Whitman's Calamus poems with those from his Children of Adam. Where the body in Calamus is incessantly hidden, metaphorized as leaves, roots, blossoms, scented herbage, live oak, moss, vines and buds, now it can be revealed in its polymorphous glory as arms, shoulders, lips, fingers, loins, elbows and necks. No more will we hear—as in Calamus—"I dare not tell it in words" or "Here I shade and hide my thoughts;" rather, as in Children of Adam: "Be not afraid of my body."

It seems essential to me, in the age of AIDS, to keep the body forward, to keep the parts named, to not let ourselves get scared back into our various closets by those who would profit from sexual repression, from sublimation and fear

of sex. What losses do we suffer by blindly embracing—
if not "compulsive" sex—compulsive dating, compulsive
monogamy, compulsive matrimony and domesticity, and
when does avoidance of particular sex acts deteriorate into
avoidance of creative exploration: dulled nerves, consumer-
ist complacency, couplist or nuclear family paranoia, social
scapegoating, stereotyping and moral sanctimony? Didn't
my generation become sexual pioneers not just by increas-
ing the range of permissible sex acts and sex-enacted places but by tying sexual expression to socialism, feminism,
national liberation movements, consciousness expansion,
legal and individual rights and radical psychologies, and if
it gets squashed what else gets squashed with it? The cha-
otic force of eros—once called *desire*—is a depth charge for
change. Contain it and we may live an ordered existence,
sure: *following* orders.

So I do *not* propose "City of Men," or any other creative
act, as a substitution for sex. I do of course propose safe
sex—*medically* safe but not politically safe, not socially or
even psychically safe. And toward the day when the Human Immunodeficiency Virus is consigned to the dustbins
of history, I'll dream—with Whitman—"Unscrew the locks
from the doors!/ Unscrew the doors themselves from their
jambs!"

(1988)

Notes from Under

It is alphabetic from the start, as if the full name were too terrible to be spoken, or because we don't want to know the elaboration that would cause a true and necessary engagement with its nature; prefer a modest, even pleasant-sounding acronym to keep it hidden: AIDS. And so it remains a shark fin disease, barely indicated above, red maw gaping beneath the sight line—for those, that is, who live—marginal—beneath the infested sea. If you live here, you know it. If not, have you heard the drowning screaming your names? If not, what constitutes your privilege, and how will you receive my anger?

I am not, here, talking sex, though certainly that sublime loss of self has been threatened with—at least—self-consciousness. I have been immersed in a more quotidian terror, its brunch and coffee dialogues, or dream analogues, or telephone weepings; in community (the Gay, though clearly others are affected—all are affected—the community of affected I know are Gay) conversation, its local pits and searing elevations. So, a cloud of attendant issues and their griefs. Among friends—dead, dying, or scared, the sorrowful healthy—testimony: what I have seen that you must now know, see, for I have been surrounded and among my friends in adversity creating a life, their rising and falling beauties, deaths and tests and imagined fulfilled acts that have unleashed instructions upon us, the uninitiated.

*

For this, reading the world, new language events by which we measure grief and fear; how the virus has made us talk about it—forms of disclosure, witness, vocabularies, stories. A new literary structure I feared becoming master of: the obituary. One's sense of the vanishing, people and—struggle against it as we will (buried alive!)—era. How what we look for first, almost perverse in eagerness, in the Gay weekly papers are the names and photos of those who've died this week. Who and how many did you know, numbers as stripes of honor. "I knew five people this week." And I didn't even know T had been sick till I saw his photo in the obituaries—a thrill with which one engages the paper, surprise building toward their appearance on page 12, to see how much sorrow one can translate into endurance. And cry, continually, because some lover used a nickname for his dead friend—*and* direct address—and it's hard to be impersonal when people are calling each other sweetie across *that* gulf. (I can't—don't want to—say the names of endearment here; I/thou is their only proper usage; what signifies is that the form functions while including the dead.) And, as adjunct language, there are lists: how as a young man—a baby homosexual, I say—I kept a tally of the first men I laid, on one hand (with names), two hands, too many for fingers and toes, finally uncountable. Then, around 1982, the list began of who had died, who sick, who sero-positive—soon, too, uncountable. Another fear: the fear of forgetting. With its shadow: the desire to forget.

I'm infected by a vocabulary, a prisoner of its overspecialized agenda. I know OK-T4 helper cells, macrophages, lymphadenopathy, hairy leukoplakia; I know the syntax— the route of congregation—more than the definitions. By how they appear in the sentence I can pretty much tell what the end is going to be. I read their appearance on the body of a text and get its message. I see a sign which means one of these words is going to insist on being used: He's walking with a cane—probably had pneumocystis; what's that spot on his neck— Kaposi's sarcoma? He forgot what he just said—dementia? His hair has that peculiar thinness, he looks weak, pale, lost, tired, ruddy. (He looks better—taking AL721? He's gaining weight—from AZT?) Did I have a night sweat, a cough, a fever; am I weak, tired, pale, out of breath; what's that white stuff on my tongue—thrush? Am I in or out of control? I'm learning this alien vocabulary by sight—it's symbolic—but I don't understand the grammar. I can't apply it to any other situation; it's a purely local dialect. Desperate, I use these medical words as markers, to chart the distance between my body and absolute fear, or my body and the hope of health—represented as control by the command of Scientific Terminology and its promise.

We have conversations in various forms whose essence

is *disclosure*. One is sero-positive or negative, another has just been diagnosed. The build-up to announcement along a route of suspense: Sit down, I have some bad news, X got . . . , or Did your hear about . . . ; more and more minimal overtures to stage the news, down to a single dolorously inflected, "Well . . ." (I told J about L and—as I expected—he cried hard. D said, "You got to bust his cherry.") We terrorize each other with the news, we get giddy and push our desperation toward the small comfort of The Absurd, staged as impossible excess. We take tests, and friends hold our hands as we receive the word which threatens to define us, to force us into the duty of its own replication. It's dry; the word burns out of control. His news precedes him: scent on the wind. (I'd heard about S but I hadn't seen him yet. When I did see him I asked him, "How are you feeling?" He looked at me—about to disclose his diagnosis—tilted his head quizzically—then realized because I'd asked not How *are* you but How are you *feeling,* that I already knew.) Sometimes we know things about each other we didn't want each other to know—whispers and hand-me-down disclosures—and we are even *friends*—but we know that vocabulary in the hands of others creates stigma, grows in the social body as the virus grows in the physical. "Positive" and "negative" becomes signs not just for our physiological trials but for civil restrictions, and in these matters we are rarely wrong in trusting our deepest paranoias. (On our first date, W—handsome, warm, mature, sexy—told me he had mild symptoms of ARC [AIDS-related complex]. My desire was confounded, cauterized at the source. He left feeling embarrassed and somehow guilty; I left embarrassed, guilty, and ashamed.)

And the demand to hear the voice of concern, magic words, from my—especially—"straight" friends, and to voice back, continually, to those I know are ill: How are you (feeling)? To care to ask; dare to find out. And be prepared to listen to the litany of fear, rage, loss, disease; to be an open ear, organ of sympathy. And if someone passes, be witness, give testimony, tell stories, name names. Yes, I am well, but I am surrounded by a quilt of names (The Names Project— over 8,000 commemorative panels sewn together)—a comforter—creating among a congress of the dead a community of the bereaved. First names and last names, nicknames and drag names ("We miss you girlfriend"), alongside the artifactual evocations of kinship and culture: ball gowns, leather jackets, teddy bears, rodeo boots, political buttons, snapshots, and glitter—and the interpolation of desire read as care, the carefulness with which a quilt my many hands is being stitched into a poetics of loss. This, on a panel:

His love came at me like a river. I felt so inadequate as
    though I were trying to catch it all in a tin cup.

God bless you Luis. May god allow me to stand before
    you when next you open your beautiful Spanish eyes.

*

Some are able, we have seen, to tell: to live out their evictions as full tenancy and shock us with what they understand of what we can barely see. In the midst of this all I saw my literal father die, faint expirations, fainter than any he'd ever before taken, round little puffs he blew like smoke rings from his cheeks, five or six only, lighter than air. The macho bull exited like the sweetest ballet fairy, relaxed at last, softspoken, delicate. Some men I've seen—how do they do it?—I don't know—and only some have—live sharper, richer, after diagnosis, become bigger, more generous (and not just the context) as they become thinner and weaker, have found a calmness unsettling but calming to those around them, so fine is their strength and so little do the rest of us know about death, bereft of ritual, corpse, and interment, surrounded by our fears projected as the grotesque.

Eric was my good friend T's sometime lover, hence in proximity to my daily life if not exactly of it. We'd seen each other dozens of times over ten or so years, but had never really spent time together, just the two of us. He got sick and died slowly, the first I knew well to transform, to metamorphose along the disease's route of thin, thinner, thinnest. A possessor of erotic power most of his life, he never let go of it, by which I mean to say that his body never became an ugly thing, though he was radically disfigured. His desire to charm outpointed his powerful adversary. A small army of friends were his defenders, scheduling precisely his daily meetings, meals, sheet-changes, medicines, and "dish" sessions. Eric's dying was a site of empowerment. The server and the served were connected by the line of interdependence that constitutes a meaningful act. As he got sicker, T tried to draw me into this nexus of exchange; he knew the degree of care needed, knew I could be useful, and recruited me—it was for *him* I did it, as if he were the one in need of care (as, of course, he was.) I committed to feed Eric lunch on such and such a day.

I was nervous, hadn't yet confronted anyone head-on who owned the disease, wanted to be correct, polite, less fearful than I was, more comfortable than I anticipated being. First we tended to functional details, then Eric and I got down to the serious business of being casual. Almost immediately, he showed me the way. "You know," he said, "one of the nice things about being sick is that I get to see the people I like, but wouldn't ordinarily spend time with." With a swift lunge of graciousness he'd assumed the position of caregiver by putting *me* at ease, making *me* feel good. By turning the occasion away from illness and towards sociability, he located himself as a giver as well as a taker—a liver instead of a dier. Eric was *living* of AIDS.

In the end—a year or so of abstract fear, a year of diagnosis—Chuck and I were great friends. This after twelve years of community association—shared podiums, rallies, cultural events, meetings; do-gooders in our mutual minds, busybodies, respecting each other but never actually—yet—friends.

But something cut through as he got sicker, a relief, release, that led us together as if we'd really known each other during the twelve years we sort of had. We grew old together in a year and a half—with the shared vision of ethnic cultural kin—like East Coast Old World Jews in our Miami rockers. We laughed a lot (given the situation), criticized and critiqued, argued, and basked in the easiness of our longterm newfound alliance. How did he make me continue to feel he was cute—"a doll"—I did—even as he grew frail, emaciated, at once bony and soft—like a monkey, I said—his evaporation process seemed sweet even as I cursed it.

This is the very tiny part of the story I want to tell: M said he thought Chuck was beginning to show signs of dementia—final terror down the road of struggle when you can't even form the idea of "courage" to bear you forward—and this was a rumor that prickled all our skins. It was Thanksgiving; on my way to the country I was to drop off for Chuck some of my Turkey Day prizes: Viennese Marzipan Bars, with homemade almondcake bottoms, apricot jelly layers, and bittersweet chocolate tops. I didn't want to be feeding them to Chuck-who-wouldn't-know-where-he-was. I was scared, though I hadn't myself seen any indications to confirm the rumor—but really how many space-outs would it take to signal the onset? Ah, my doll, my girlfriend-in-arms from the old days anyway, my honest dignified teacher, as I trepidatiously entered your room that day not knowing what to expect—this weird ironic American harvest ritual—you called to me from across your bed, your boat out in a few days, with full holiday spirit called to me cheerily across the room, "Bird-Girl!" By which I knew you knew it was the day of stuffed turkey, that it was a good and a horrible day, that we were "dolls" together speaking in code, and that you were a "queen" in full un-demented possession of her essential ironic distance.

Then—O True Bird Girl—you flew away.

Long blond hair, flowy clothes—this was in 1974 when I met him—an impeccable sense of colors and their dream coordinates, handsome with real bone structure, and even literary smarts. Everyone knew, could *see*, Jackson was a renaissance man; he could do *everything* (except maybe relax)—at that time weaving hand-spun and -dyed clothing, and writing a little poetry. But *Design* would cover my sense of his power: the ability to place things in juxtaposition— objects or threads—so that their uniqueness was set into resonance—like a tuning fork—each unit or strand or line brought into active consonance with the others, a poem. I should say that when he died a year ago, after struggling with AIDS lymphatic cancer, and he had long since ceased to be the modelly beauty of yore—though testimony to his personal power and insight even increased (and I saw it in his person which I couldn't name a "corpse" only hours after he died—he was strong, present—electric even— his constellation absolutely in order)—I gazed at his body floating in bed, but couldn't help noticing, also, the books on the nearby shelves—how they were *arranged,* some on

their side, some standing, some leaning—in a precise balance—the objects on the side table too—and I admired, en-
vied that order which nailed the exact image of casualness,
composition, and serenity: the material world in luscious
objectivist presence.

But his wound had opened—unhealed open "mouth" on
his neck from a gland that hadn't quite been excised (the
"mouth of hell" I thought) that he wrapped in his own famous scarves but couldn't keep closed. Once and then twice
it ruptured that morning, hemorrhaged so that he could see
he would be swept away in its profusion of blood. And so he
asked C, his lover and primary caregiver, to carry him into
the garden so he could "bleed into the earth." "Let me bleed
into the earth." Jackson was able to arch over his death this
worshipful poetic figure, to guide as communion a passing
that others would read as being taken away. Blood streaming around him like a heroine's hair, Jackson arranged his
last words, and put the world in order. Who knew that a
man could have such precise integrity in that particular
moment, could engage his death *actively*—with cognizance
and will—as a life image, could make of his final moments
not a destruction but a creative act?

*

My friends reading these drops on paper, of this, now I am
sure: We can die with our hats on, we can die with our boots
on, we can call ourselves by name as we enter the rolls, we

can pierce the ground and draw in the dust—in the dust of ourselves!—on dissolving knees—the complex design of our presence and release.

(1988)

The Depositories

The enemy personified the nation. A fiction or series of fictions exploding through with smoke, pouring sweat. At the foot of a tree hands stuck in the dirt. Once in a while they hold on to me.

A couple of them seemed to be moving around the field, black-eyed, loose splinters from the neighborhood, full of wasted determination. He coughed it up on the pillow in a sort of puddle. The forms lying there, vacant, removed from there.

The house thin, blue, hanging in the air, transparent in the trees, the forms of the trees, no partition whichever way you move . . .

This man was weak, received a box from home, munching on a bloody cracker in the remaining hand. Two boatloads arriving, exposed to it anywhere, torches on the ground, rags around heads, hot at night with sudden energy, the maintaining skin of vengeance. Green oozing out from the grass—large spaces swept over—burning the dead beards, odor of the rejected arm and leg. In history the paper remain and still remain, soaking up the glaze . . .

I sit by his shining hair, the heart of the stranger. His ashy eyes, roasted in the morning. As you pass by, be on guard where you look. Opposite my window the freed horses are led off. The smoke streams upward, dark, thick, warm.

He said, "Make your own choice." The kiss I gave him discharged better views.

The man is struggling for breath; a soldier's life must be a bent thing. Others are arranged in a straight row. They have some old magazines I was in the habit of reading: theory, practice, democratic premises, superfluity. He was an ideal of his age in a few days. He kept a diary and wrote, "The doctors have been brave."

I am taking care of a silent rebel, laid down on his arm to see its distribution, lying on the spot that time a hole in the air, his small calculations extruded. Meat might be named from mere demonism; nature and pretense were there.

I like to stand and look a long while. Individuals in human places verify the forms. The dim leaden members with heads leaning and voices speaking. In the arms and in the legs from my observation.

Dear Madame, I have seized the testimony, still alive. I do not know his past life, but feel as if it must have been good.

I saw circumstances, and can give you some fragmentary physiognomy and idioms . . .

Flesh of his breast and tremulous arms in the strain of a partial sleep, I have a special friend. Out of the shadowy scene the white beds, sat by a huddled form, shone in through the window a vacant moon . . .

Buttons . . . tufts of hair . . .
In bushes, low gullies, or on the sides of hills . . .

(1989)

Strips And Streamers

One had forces marching in silence—the most venom-
ous kind—without intermission, smashed like a bitter
plate—Napoleonic colonels had made their title clear.
Something begins—frozen hard—even a mattress—with
the men—such as it is—helpless on the field, the city
worse—have burst from the wounds a telegraphic message to get well.

Right through the bladder and coming back out—Washing-
ton waters with all its features—entering us like a wedge—
through the helpless foliage, flashes of fire, crashing men,
groans in an open space with the fresh smell of blood blown
off the face or head—amid the woods, masses, mortal purposes up there, a few stars.

Is sleeping soundly at this moment, a hole straight through
the lungs. He lies naked—the stimulants of every object
bleached from his cheeks—the strangeness of perfect hair,
green eyes—hold onto my hand—ashy apple—shot in the
head with a few words, wants nothing, emanating artillery
and slow blows of axes.

Some piles of men—thick pontoons—dripping their handsome faces, superfluous flesh.

You desire him. There hangs something. His absence.

The space near it looked like the sky, specimens of un-worldliness.

The men may have been odd, but they fell before me like a murmur. Each has his peculiarities with blank paper—doctrine, confession, recitation; the problem is to organize principles out of it; present struggle: tender waste.

He was among the first fighting. He lived three days, so that the brains lay there in the open air. Their backs were in different parts of their bodies, inscriptions pinned to their breasts. In places you have this opportunity. He died yesterday.

I walked home about sunset. A boy called to me. I stood impassive as my stupid eye just occurred.

Some had blankets around their shoulders—strips and streamers and meat—through the long apartments—former winters—to follow his passionate action in a subtle world of air—a different sunlight, full of whirling rage—long, long before they were due.

Without parallel, down to this hour. There have been samples of another description, but his eyes will never be written.

From the glowing prostration and the marrow of constant rain.

[1990]

Further Under

Ten years later of unnamed terrors and specific losses, AIDS comes closer into my life in waves, "waves of nearness", raising its shark fin in my direction, then circling farther. The blood-scented waters could make one pass out . . .

Some, of course, do pass out—right out of the circle. But if anything besides rage is clear in these drowning surroundings, it's the clarity of those few who seem to quicken in their sickness and dying, those gifted few who stay awake as they fall away, and offer to us attendant comrades instructions from the beyond, or the going-beyond.

It may be my own voracious sentimentality and romantic yearning that seek to transform these bitter passages into something more informed. Yes, well, but I've had at least serious co-conspirators who've given me my figures, phrases, mantras, mudras, holy dish . . .

*

Leland was well into ten years of ardent Tibetan Buddhist studies when his first KS lesions appeared, and had already weathered crises in his new ancient faith. He'd left a live-in ashram in an attempt to localize, individualize the mind-stilling Buddhism he craved (as he'd sought even before AIDS to still a sex-crave that kept him ever hungry, in

Buddhist terms a "hungry ghost"). But abstinence of flesh wasn't for him; he had a more modest—and grander—goal of achieving fleshly pleasure without gnawing the bone, of finding a serene balance right here in his quirky gay life of theater, theatricality, drama, and drama queens. So when AIDS announced its way through his body he was already troubling himself into a distinctly American—one might say San Franciscan—Buddhism.

As he began to sicken and die, he kept his eye hard on the process, informed by ritual precepts I can't repeat for being uninformed. He watched his body as if it were *a* body—*The* body—and tracked in his agitated mind the one purposeful Mind. If it sounds high-minded it sounded so to Leland too: he was constantly failing. He was constantly succeeding and failing.

In between hospital visits, over a home-cooked meal, he detailed the problem to me. He was using mantras and other self-awareness exercises to quiet his thinking. "But every time I get to a certain place—a level—and think I'll be able to relax into stillness," he complained agitatedly, "I start to hear the theme from 'Bonanza'—*Bonanza!*—and can't concentrate!" He looked more than frustrated: tried, tested, chagrined. "There it is, so ridiculous. I try to dismiss it and can't relax." He saw the irony in his dilemma, but was nevertheless exasperated, stopped at the threshold—*and he was trying to die well*—by this paradigm of idiot chatter. He couldn't break through.

It seemed to me that as long as you had an idea of "breaking-through" you weren't being, or accepting, where you were. But young John, cleaning Leland's kitchen, put it to him more gracefully. "If I got to that place," he shrugged, "and I heard the theme from 'Bonanza', I'd just start singing it." His Buddhist lesson was simple: Go with it. Sing 'Bonanza'! This natural comprehension charmed Leland completely. He was humbled and thrilled and knew John was right. Was he even a little shaken such direct understanding came from someone unschooled in the lore, cracking an already shaky belief in the doctrinaire forms he'd been studying? I don't know if he actually took to singing the theme song, but that mundane media riff lodged in his mind opened a door. He began to gain the courage to transform Buddhism to his own specifics of a mid-life Hollywood-bred theater-tenured brilliant quirky awkwardly frustrated subtly flamboyant queen dying of AIDS in 1990 San Francisco.

Nesting uncomfortably in his last hospital bed, he told me of the new trouble he was having with one of his former ashram mates, who felt him straying from the Way, and was raising alarms, making him feel like a Bad Boy. Having struggled through 30 years of homo sex-guilt to find some measure of peace-of-mind-in-body, Leland found bad-Buddhism death-guilt not very attractive. Tibetan was beginning to turn him off. The ornate, symbolic Thanka paintings he'd actually helped print in America were starting to seem alien, exo-cultural. Who were the Bodhisattvas to him in California; what in Tibetan spoke to his idiosyncratic world? He wanted to die, he explained to me, governed by the things that already mattered to him, that came directly out of his life, ritualized by early investment and repetition, then fixed in the firmament for guidance. Could these even be his own *theatrical* icons, long ago installed: Elizabeth Taylor, the Trembling Bountiful, or Barbra Streisand, the swan-voiced Yearning Duck?

As he spoke his mood was growing more excited and defiant. He was coming to a vision of "grace", informed by the sublimely silly creatures of the gay quotidian, suffered, nurtured, transcended, and adored. "Barbra Streisand songs *are* my mantras," he squealed heretically. "They're what I know by heart, what I already repeat and repeat." This was too good. I glanced at the photo of Liz he'd tacked on the hospital wall. Fresh from the bath in her ripe-skinned middle period, she gazed serenely—unabashedly—from beneath a pink towel done up as a turban. All she lacked for true diva status was a jewel in the forehead. "Here's your goddess, your Tara," I said—Liz didn't blink—and we howled. Something had been transformed. The daily world one lived in had sprouted its own golden feathers. Leland had found his rhythm, and started to relax.

The next day I brought him a homemade tape of Streisand's second and third albums—the songs we both knew well—had, in fact, grown up together singing—and on which Streisand's voice still maintains jazz inflections, a girlish purity of sexual longing, and a mature woman's saturation of sexual fulfillment and loss. This time, though, the clear plastic box read, "Barbra Streisand Sings Tibetan Buddhist

Chants", while on the tape itself was printed, modestly, "Babs sings Buddhism."

*

I'm a reporter, I see now, rereading this tale. Ten years of AIDS has altered my poetic gift, narrowed my eye, humbled my language. What do I know about death except what my friends have shown me—I let *them* speak—for what did I know before, a virgin, uninitiated, unendured? Death's literalness is what I've been given, and the poetics of struggle have forged from it not transcendence but enactment. That fact of acceptance—the acceptance of that fact!—lies before me like a series of steps, rigorous, unsentimental, hilarious, florid but precise . . .

*

After Leland returned home from the hospital—which he desperately wanted to do—I sat on his bed and welcomed him back. "Well, you're home, now." "Yes," he replied, "I'm home and I'm going somewhere." That process, surrounded by a vigilant circle of friends and family, brought him in and out of lucidity and strength, though never at the price of clarity. After a dip that seemed almost certainly final, he rebounded. Thin and frail and blemished, he dished through some photos with J and me. Then, in what was the last detailed conversation we had (aside from my explaining to joyous him that the life-support system was being withdrawn) Leland, with the exacting eye of a critic, and the forgiving eye of a fan, and the third overarching eye of a born director, explained to us, barely audible, rasping and gulping the words, the precise differences between Angela Lansbury's and Tyne Daley's interpretations of Rose in "Gypsy." No more fear now of having Inappropriate Mind. If "Rose's Turn" was the theme-song at hand, it would be embraced. Did he *perform* it?—I can't remember—it seems to me he sang all the songs. And it seemed to me that this being-who-he-was to the end was validation for all he'd been before, indicated the peace and acceptance he'd rigorously struggled to achieve.

He died quietly the next morning. When I arrived at his house a few hours later, I peeked into his room, saw the flattened covers where I expected a mound, and was surprised that his body had already been whisked away. It seemed too soon. I talked with gathering friends. One asked if I'd gone to sit with the body. "But it isn't there; I looked; they already took it away." In fact, I was told—"But I looked!"— his body *was* still there; I glanced back through the door— where? Then I noticed, collapsed beneath the blankets as if air alone had sustained it, now exhaled, deflated, one-tenth of its former size, a few barely noticeable bumps raising the covers, the suggestion of Leland's body. The rest had vanished, puff of smoke. It was hard to believe someone had been there; it was hard to believe something was there now.

I didn't look.

*

The little decisions people make create the one AIDS narrative that keeps me sane. I'm made to understand the meticulous dimensions of life lived thoroughly by those in the process of losing it. Ken, gaunt and bruised, whose dying radiated power, who shared a very purposeful half-hour with me two days before he died (though I was really his lover's friend and hadn't known him intimately); sharing just enough time, I think he thought, to educate me, to let me feel his acute mind and sharp will issuing from utterly ravaged body. Ken, who thanked me for coming, and when I answered, on exit, "No, thank *you*," threw back in a clear voice, instantaneous and unaffected, accepting my acknowledgment without vanity, "You're welcome." Ken's body—which I *did* look at—hands bent backwards touching beneath his chin in a death mudra laid out by his lover, impossibly unnatural in life, winged articulate in death, his tightened face eyes wide open—having seen the Virgin Mary come to take him, flaming sword and heart—gazing up and out, open gazing, open gazing . . .

Or young John, desperately thinning, in a burst of exuberance donning a pink and turquoise sun dress, blond curly wig, sunglasses, and blue kerchief, vamping on my couch and rug like the skeleton of Nancy Reagan (but Nancy Reagan *is* the skeleton of Nancy Reagan!), utilizing both his body and his loss-of-body, exhibiting outrageously what I might call not *joie de vivre* but *joie de mourir*.

Or Ken again, emaciated in bed, booming a voice from what hidden reservoir?, in a chamber of tropical plants, chants from an unseen tape recorder wafting like smoke through the room, like wind at the door, with a clear luscious photo on the nightstand of a hidden beach, long and curvacious. "Is that in Hawaii?" I asked. "No, it's in New Zealand, near my friends' house." I knew he loved the talismanic sea. "Have you been there?" "No," he answered carefully, "Not yet . . ."

(1991)

Orphée
The Kiss of Death

The poet falls in love with the world and constantly dies for it—circle of frenzy and release—*Orphée!* Or the poet expires so that his (her) words may live [is that the same as not having a social life?]. He falls literally into the hands of L'Amour La Mort. Orphée (Jean Marais) and his Death (Maria Casarès) stalk each other. Their primal attraction is poetic divination and fate, seen in love's mirror as mutual fire-in-the-eyes. "It's not about understanding; it's about belief." Expectant, vain, exalted, Orpheus takes his lover's vow, poet's creed: "Toujours?" "Je jure." The rhyme of 'always' and 'I swear', oath of eternal enactment, is the same for artist and lover: to go *all the way* through the mirror's veil. "Say forever."

For Cocteau the drama's a Parisian romance played out between pompadour and high heels. The scene borrows glamour from Hollywood to push the metaphor and make it itch: The eternal oath is sealed with a hot kiss. She's in two-piece wasp-waist Escoffier and he's all jawline and blond raked hair. Where earlier the radio of inspiration might have been the muse's wellspring, now it's background music to an embrace. Casarès lights a cigarette. "Do you love this man?" demands the judge. Casarès exhales, says nothing. Insistent, "Do you love this man?" "Oui." Orphée swells and gasps; Death's black gloves and pearls. Alone in the adjacent room—"Mon amour"—they touch; they kiss. They fall to the bed. Casarès's teardrop face—pointed chin and radically upswept eyes like Satan herself—is bathed in light. They lie down forever and swear.

After fifteen years and perhaps a dozen viewings, I'm watching the movie again with my students, having offered to initiate them into Cocteau's mystery: the resonant unfolding charm of perfect metaphor, each side ceaselessly amplifying the other. This is the heart of the movie, the scene that's always held me in thrall, Death explaining the universal chain of command that I've read as Creative Order, the order of Form calling the poet to work: "transmitted by so many messengers that it's like the tom-toms of your African tribes, the echoes of your mountains, the wind in the leaves of your forests." But this time I'm feeling weak at the knees; something new in the scene disturbs me—I feel oddly embarrassed, *shocked*. I'm pulled out of the poetics and land in the purely transgressive nature of the kiss: unsettling, scandalous. He's kissing *death*. It may seem moody and romantic but he's *making love to death* . . .

Why am I so unbalanced now by this familiar scene? [D.H. Lawrence: "Why does the thin grey strand/ Floating up from the forgotten/ Cigarette between my fingers,/ Why does it trouble me?// Ah, you will understand . . ."] These well-worn words have redefined themselves: kiss of death, The Kiss of Death. How altered my sense of this stock phrase, how literal its reinvention . . . How fearfully, now, behind each stolen kiss; how courageously behind each true one . . . How familiar death has become in my casual life; how complexly my friends have embraced it. Ah, you will understand . . . AIDS . . . AIDS.

For now overlaid upon Cocteau's poetic myth is a real kiss, newly fabled. My old friend Marshall is nursing his dying lover, Ken. The frame cannot be bleached of Ken's wilful blue sores, skeleton-haunted body, feverish lips. Hollywood lighting will not erase the shadow in his cheeks, ashen tinge of skin. In a pale room, on a San Francisco hill, the morning before Ken dies, his lover's oath continues: "I love you baby." To his mother: "This is my farewell kiss to you." To Marshall, eagerly, "Kiss me, baby." Ken doesn't have the advantage of a cinched black dress and pearls. He's wearing padded hospital diapers, pulling them down because he feels they're not sexy. He says to Marshall, "Suck my lizard tongue." Marshall does.

I'm shaking in the juncture of Cocteau's spirit-zone and my friend's house. Do actual death and disease derange the vital romance of this lived "scene"; do they disgust and terrorize, black out the spotlight, stop the radio? I've seen in the announcement of this true kiss a hail of blisters, spiral rashes, white spots on the tongue, thin lusterless hair, sunken cough-wracked chests, purple swollen noses, fading eyes, parched throats. In my work, at my desk, on the tip of my pen, on your lips, on your tongue—I see Jackson's distended lymphatic neck, Eric's giant eyes, Iolo's broken walk, Chuck's pushing skull, Leland's loose-pulling skin.

These are the images that would stop the kisses, silence the poem. They don't stop Marshall, who's met his fate in Ken's love, not in his death. Whose oath takes him within the failing heart of his beloved, and beats *there*. Marshall, who delivers a fearless kiss in the transfixed zone where death's permanence lets love keep living.

Before encountering *his* death, Orpheus is dead-tired, his form has gone flat. Celebrity has leeched from his work the edge of daring. He *pleases*. "Orpheus . . .your most serious defect is knowing just how far one can go," but no farther. In the words transmitted from the zone by dead Cegeste and the Princess—discrete surreal phrases and the formal purity of numbers—Orpheus rediscovers his passionate disequilibrium. He pushes through to a place he doesn't understand but believes in, down through the layers and accretions of mud, language, faces in the mirror, beloved's glances, worn rhythms to an intuited measure found in a black and pure embrace.

The poet meeting his fate in poetry, the lover in loving: propriety serves neither, both must go too far. In that rapturous clasp of Orphée and his death I recognize the grip of devotion, the intent out of bounds, the pure *work*. [Robert Duncan: "Our uses are our illuminations."] Throughout the Zone—"memories of men and the ruins of their habits"—and haunting the house, mere information restrains hand and heart, the giving and the art. Many are abandoned by those unwilling to go far *enough*. "Will it be easier if I say goodbye?" asks Marshall, standing there. "Yes," answers

Ken, "Say goodbye." And here the kiss of death is love's wound healed by love's avowal.

PRINCESS I must leave you, but I swear I'll find a way for us to be united.

ORPHEUS Say "forever."

PRINCESS Forever.

ORPHEUS Swear to it.

PRINCESS I swear.

(1992)

Turn Around
A Solo Dance with Voice

for John B. Davis, born 1964, died 1992 of AIDS

first performed by Ney Fonseca for Juntos Dance, 10/2/92

PART 1

OFF-STAGE VOICE John looked down at himself lying there: the sunken cheeks, the shaved skull, the thin light body curled on its side in bed, almost hovering. He was so detached he wanted to sketch himself from above: the curves and hollows of his boned-on muscles, the blooming fluid in his skin. He would put the drawing in a frame that was a box and that will have been him, finished. John looked down at the hospital room and the window and the people crouched there, the pink stucco building and the boulevard of eucalyptus trees. He looked as the park as it . . .

NEY FONSECA I hate this story!

VOICE It's a true story.

NEY I'm sick of it.

VOICE He was a friend of yours.

NEY It's the same story.

VOICE Well, each one is different.

NEY The same one!

The same goddam same one fucking same one shit same one.

VOICE Should I tell you a different one?

NEY Yes.

VOICE Another story?

NEY Yes.

VOICE OK. Ney Fonseca looked down at himself lying there. He floated above the tiny body that seemed to float on the bed, brittle and frail . . .

NEY That's not fair!

VOICE . . . he said.

NEY THAT'S NOT FAIR!

VOICE It's not a story about fairness.

NEY I won't listen.

VOICE . . . he said . . .

NEY Stop that!
  I'm not listening.

VOICE I already have your ears.

NEY I won't watch.

VOICE I've already taken your eyes.

Pause

NEY Tell me again, then.

VOICE This is a story about becoming a story. It has to be
  told. It has to be put in the past.

NEY . . . he said . . .

VOICE It's a story about becoming the past . . .

NEY It has to be told.

VOICE It has to pass through. Telling turns it around. It doesn't disappear . . .

NEY It turns around . . .

VOICE It begins again and it turns around . . .

NEY It turns into the past . . ,

VOICE . . . he said . . .

NEY . . . looking down at himself lying there . . .

VOICE . . . the heat and the sex and even the dance washed from him . . .

NEY . . . the heat . . . and the sex . . . and even the dance washed from me
watching myself
lying there.

PART II

OFFSTAGE VOICE Hey, John, I just heard some new Chopin; it's a little piece called "Berceuse."

["Berceuse" begins.]

[Lines spoken at 20 second intervals over music as the dancer moves . . .]

John Doll, I found a video of this woman playing the Debussy Etudes, and then talking about them.

*

Johnny-Pie, are you going to the lake party tomorrow?

*

Hey Doll, did you talk to Jeffrey? We're going to see Cocteau's *Orpheus* on Wednesday.

*

Johnny Mae, I heard you were talking to a young blond at the café. Hmmm?

*

JohnEEE, can I borrow that tape of Aprile Millo on the radio? And you have to come see the video of *Ballo in Maschera*.

*

Hey Doll, I taped the Nijinsky "Right of Spring."

*

John, which Cocteau Twins albums do you have?

*

Johnny-Pie, I got a huge Rembrandt book you have to see.
All the paintings and the etchings.

*

Hey John, want to go to Opera in the Park with me and
Weissman and Adrian?

*

John, do you still have those tickets to see Ney dance at the
Herbst? I do wanna go.

*

Hey Doll . . .
. . . How are you feeling . . . ?

PART III

Wordless movement, ending with spins.

(1992)

A Lull in the Void
Postscript to "Turn Around"

I'm driving up highway 101 north—spring fields of yellow mustard and those *positioned* cattle—toward beloved Harbin Hot Springs to burn off some work-related tensions. My Chopin (he's *mine!*) is on the tape deck, a compilation of "Impromptus" and singularities, the last remaining Chopin unfamiliar to me. Suddenly that delicate "Berceuse" begins (its feet barely touch the ground), a few lightly swaying notes and I'm plunged—I'll be plunged forever—into Ney's dance for our friend John, dead at 28 of AIDS.

My text that goes with this music (Part II of the dance, "Turn Around") addresses John through a range of endearments *(Johnny-Pie!)*, inviting him to share the kind of art/events our friendship reveled in—an eclectic spread that spoke to the absolute delectation of cultural education, and had as its undertow—big sister to little sister—the Passing of the Lore: because I'm an official Old Queen now (I subscribe to the opera) and he was a baby one (a taste for Debussy preceded by a devotion to Barbra Streisand). I thought I had completed a gesture (I thought Ney had completed a gesture), but hearing "Berceuse" today brings John's death back with a vengeance. We spin in circles to maintain equilibrium. (Ney swirls Part III of the dance in a centrifugal white skirt.)

Norma said lately I've been looking good, *seeming* good. I attribute this new sheen to purposeful employment and to what I'm calling a lull in the void: nobody close to me has died recently. It's a small grace, and fragile; it can turn around. This man John who was really a boy to me, who was so young to me, little brother or little sister, this Johnny-Pie is last year's passing. (It was several months after writing Part II that I found out 'berceuse' means 'lullaby.')

Death is so *open!* My writing's unequal to the task of bringing John back to life (his contradictions alone were too breathtaking!) but his dying returns to me, regularly, a restless farewell loop . . . There's a movement Ney does over Chopin's music—you should see it. It's tiny, a lateral sway, a shuffle to the side like a blown leaf. It's what I was listening for today . . . a little music to rest the dead . . . or *lullaby* in the void . . .

(1993)

Human Immune

I lie in your arms. I kiss your mouth. Use your nails, creature. Our roles—the crown, the infractions—inhabit this sanctified place to the point of fanaticism. I have to get my hands on the world.

Dead from complicity in San Francisco discharged me, the harp of a person had an arc. Then listen to inhale the contagion, where in the trap of your consciousness you have to pull to get out. Himself alone and scared kill mercies. The body has powers to paint yourself purple.

And shifting grasses, such erosion and mosses, nightjars lived on the droppings of sunny days . . . in that country of circumstances and moods—shattering its bark and throwing pieces of it around. Facing away from the entrance, with jerky movements kicking the sands backwards. I saw the size of a hand, losing hold of it . . .

Birdmen, across the rising hills and bay, rolling naked one night stirred and rose to the spell. He's out there, into the dead stumbling mind. I'll be accounting for no memory, without so much as a template. His nostril is hissing; his tongue in spasms. He has several parts on a breeze, an

asylum this story surrounded. The face ripping wide open
has led a team of men in white gowns and slow rhythm.

And twinges we ourselves devise woundingly by miscalcu-
lation—delicious conflagration winking—to become familiar and to pulverize them all. Curves could hope to find in
this world no more beautiful hair. *Hell is round.* I squirted
them with kisses. On his back at the edge of the couch to
die of pleasure, kneeling into your asshole to form around
me. Comprise our friends the memory of the moments they
passed in that virtue. Their honor therein, helpless before
desire . . .

Where are you now, the harder you pull to get out? Then
is that person fixing little sandwiches and watching TV?
The Bay was fucked—ornate theories—there's the previ-
ous photo of "husband", hippies, Pt. Reyes beach, leering
face, pink light, someone else. A portion of scripture, un-
diagnosed. The placement of objects is a language theme,
no longer private. A little old hairless man had swollen up.
Pain is healing me into submission, he wrote in his journal
the secret of the universe: *hell is round.* You flop and thrash
in fact.

The homecoming was marked and mapped; they circled in
ever widening loops. Processions migrating on blue nec-
tar—stopping in the rising air over coastal waters. I waited
I repeated I waited the test. The results were not fooled. I

spent the summer as a natural landmark—the bearer of delicate organs—leaving the destiny dormant on dry days—moving my wooden ship to research, under spell of the spray. The sun was gigantic, slow, low-hanging. We had to acquire some knowledge in this year, food for a narrative. Summer is short. Inquiry raising our eyebrows was contagious. Moonlight on meat.

He knelt down next to me—fallen giant, empty stump. Feeling the blood pulling around my thighs, "I think it's screaming," I said. He stood barefoot, one warm leg, nest at the belt, pink wriggling sack, I wanted to run into the sun now, bristling muscular bulging animal sedated by his eyes. My body shook against him on a hot summer day, gushing to life, blood-filled, blood-dizzy. He rolled over onto his side, watching the men. A ruin. A patient. Overgrown so that the flat air had no answer. We floated in which the memory moving our bellies going dark have all taken flight—a cure may be possible—tell me what words mean—pleasure for a coffin: turn and enter your home.

The ghost which leads to burning incense on the altars of magical friends—these gods come upon gods which erects them—confections of the deific—showers down events, the smooth operations of insignificant romances to penetrate into their historian's hearts and foist upon the reader authenticity of the marvels . . . At last he dies, this exceptional man who loves them, phantom spawn, fraudulent cures, boundless poverty and the images of objects. Just a while ago I gave you attentions pure and simple. I take the oath worthy of your friendship exterminated in me. The lancing pain stuffing me with bucks and thwacks to distill soul's fuck: slip away, leave the rest to me, initiated into our mysteries . . .

With the Sixties the Seventies in Berkeley shot forward for re-play to put the spaces where he wants—stars in the universe suggest metaphysical poets—lingered in remission studying the cosmic characteristics of T-cells. Triumphant skull in the grin of his malady, whacked as he was in a feedback loop. It's necessary to interpret men compared to sleepers in a private world. Two men pass through a forest which passed for the real world. From the cardiac ward through the underground corridor to encounter arrhythmia on the cathode screen. His head, his heart, a wave-form. And he spoke his monologue directed outward from the wisdom of a body: *hell is round,* the little clay pot locked up. The dream-time of heroes trying to throw up names: California, Parsifal, Chuck . . .

Night fell and a moon showed up between peaks. We were given a welcome for centuries. Aroused by smell in their human behavior a growl in heat, with a mixture of affection and respect. A little whipping, a little touching it lightly. One sometimes hears the ice snap with a seam in the center; large numbers breeding in our district at those breathing holes. Members kill themselves, interested only in sugar. Suddenly the door was flung open, a youth tumbled in; the event we'd been preparing for changed our life entirely. To wake up to stop the alarm clock with one hand I lay on my right side facing my other—my Other Side—pressing the human places in a firm grip that woke us up in horizontal posture turned to face each other, covered with a thick blanket, the murmur of description, connected by an invisible rod as resistance fluttered back and forth.

The end of perspective, the proper shapes, blobs and pillars and singing minarets. You're a mess in the park. You're a willing dirty dog. With the sun disappearing a low fog tucked-up the air. I slept resting on the windowsill, stranger than birds. I used to be little but when we came back they were gone. Overnight to hear whatever was to be heard. With its overgrown boxed body jerking in perfect symmetry, this wizard—see what there is to see—bruised in deep breaths, and an archaeologist invited down to watch. He'd like to go from the bay to the ancient golden hills into the earth unannounced and never saying where. It was like some mechanical body secretly unstrung leaving accretions of soft dirt and mud. He kissed his waiting hand with both hands. The warm competence of the finished parts as if such machines had meaning. Touching it, the thin shell, tucked-in facing the bay may lie quiet in the dusk.

A way is opened; my initiated companions go after. Each gave his confrere the pleasure of sensations, sprawled on the stone floor. Sucking a moment of suspense into calm to savor its entirety, the combination of prick and ass and mouth, an eternity in that delirium he'll lie in your arms. Common measure in homage to fitting company. We'll make a circle *(hell is round)*, I want that energy while speaking, place yourselves close by me, excessive behavior swell discourse in proportion, the carnal prosperity of an everyday affair. It ripens and is born, having provided circumstances. Made an incision running around the head, then removed the strip of skin. Your body, the altar, on the altar. Go consult the children of love. There are minds, my friends, certain spirits, having rid themselves of vibrations, having progressed from extravagance to the speeding star, plagued in whose name passion alone dared multiply. Come—this'll serve as a bed—fuck my ass into my mouth.

This is what the dream referred to as *hell is round.* When he got out of the hospital it had the effect of wiping out history. Right now, the city was in intensive care, locked-out behind him. In the small room huge eyes flaming. His fried mind projecting on each side a sword to conquer—through the sense organs through the rain through the ward through the trembled fields of flowers as if shape had no substance through the living information completing itself. The blood of communion turning is a strange sentence. It broke through and fired experience at his head. Penetrated man penetrated himself. He was dragged through his address book deconstructed as official documents—the only way open. A limbo in lymphoma contemplated itself: he lived it, he loved himself, would love that too. He saw it spread out among us, pulled from his body. He could hardly wait to abolish himself, freeing him to go commando saving people, glommed onto another pretext in grief and love through the magical powers that underlay all his saved-up strategy . . .

I have variations about what was there: fathers, sons, and grandsons. When the sky cleared the weather superimposed corrections, noticing and recording more details. Fly to an elevated lookout post. It's my intention to describe history at the place we left them. Populations of flesh caught in our net. Of their courtship, of their species: their back was connected to display-movements fading toward the warm neck, a pirouette. Small circles this ceremony for hours on end. About the organization of behavior: some of them visited me. Animal behavior in the summer of 1956, or '76—embarrassing luxury—while we were floating on the shore or in the sea or under veils in quiet corners as the haze hanging behind us . . . Feverish outburst played havoc with their exact pose while sitting indoors, digging out of the morning for tests, returned positive results on the same day; distance . . . I've made a number of flights already—round flat discs—homing. Then my legs stopped moving altogether. Under the full microscope ferocity with nerve endings waiting I hovered, motionless, maneuvered into position.

I will see him standing, pounded, irresistible. In the dunes of my thick woolen sweater, dropped off along the western edge, panting through the indistinct sand, puncturing the middle of the farthest horizon, arms raised. Through the muscles of aching arms and legs opening on my back to the sea, wrapped in tangled sunlight staring beyond him. What I didn't think or say fill my mouth, the terrible mysteries of sleep and navigation. We're best friends ever since ever. I noticed you in class—my full attention—if given the opportunity stammering to encompass love stanzas. Have you smiled?—choreography! Are you wrapped around my waist?—cosmic winds. San Francisco the beauty can take a picture—the air around him. I lay there on the floor, dug into the trenches, throwing down his trousers, the root of bones and mud and blood. I suppose he once lived here, curled into the tails of my nightshirt. He walked past me in his undershorts, an organism. We are the owner of sight and speech. In the gray light west of the Great Highway: not even me. We sat in silence, a blanket covering his lap. If you flew by you'd see these imposters, vapors of tenderness. It could never be contained.

(1993)

My Memorial

Either the temple itself is rising—how can such massive stone columns float in the air?—or you are descending beneath the floor's bared lip, the massive floor's meter-thick lip, to an underground (underworld?) stone chamber, airless, where a man stands as if already crushed by the ceiling's weight. "The fatal stone" is set. In the deeper shadows a whisper, a rustle, alerts the man to another's presence, a partner with whom to sing *"il nostro inno di morte"* : "our hymn of death." Their voices unbounding pressure in duet will brace the stone, and turn their death house into a resonance chamber.

But you're not watching a Metropolitan Opera broadcast of *Aida.* You're here to listen to Aprile Millo and Placido Domingo (especially Aprile) sing for me. *"O terra, addio; addio, vale di pianti"* : "Oh, earth, farewell; farewell, vale of tears." Aprile will throw her Egypt-blackened face skyward—to where the sky beyond the tomb-top *would* be—and spin her voice into a silver thread—attenuated to that point where matter must become spirit—as she sees "our wandering souls fly to the light of eternal day" : *"volano al raggio dell'eterno dì."* 'Ours' in this case is hers and mine. I have died of AIDS. And this is my memorial.

Listen ceremonially to some of the music that has *meant* me—a scrapbook requiem of ever-elaborated enthusiasms, polyphonic collage. As Immense Ptah, "supreme creator," is invoked by the priestesses, the temple seems to be lowering—for the tomb must be entombed—and the final note is an Italian plea for peace, *"pace!"* Already that silvery purified note of *"al raggio"* : "the light" has escaped its mortal prison: We're singing to you from beyond the grave. ["Remember me," pleads Dido in Purcell's opera, "but ah! forget my fate;" and I keep misremembering and hear "but *don't* forget my fate."]

Ecstatic transubstantiations in song recall my fate—but wait! OK, I'm an opera queen, a drama queen, a melody queen, a moody thing (a "Thrilling Thing," says Genet), and the gay DNA in my hypothalamus or wherever has dutifully progressed me from aria to lieder, but I don't (evidently) have HIV and I haven't (yet) died. But listening and listing—splayed on the sofa—I compose my sources: as the speakers play, as the speakers *speak*, they textualize parts of a funeral service calling backwards over me. There's self-dramatization worthy of a comic book queer, here, but the grand guignol theatrics are played out on a thrusting stage larger than my small foyer. What transpires on it is multiple, choral, and the recital is repeated in terrible modulations. Light the honey-glow candles in the wall sconce (gilded oat sheaves) and sharpen your antennae toward the tufted San Francisco night. Falling notes breeze in and out of beveled-glass windows, apartment to apartment, receiver to receiver . . .

I *have* held Leland's leaf-weight hand as the blood-feeding tubes were disconnected; I wiped Johnny's morphine-hallucinating forehead as if to clear away the false images (though it was his sister who changed his diapers); I read aloud as Chuck's dropsied brain finished my sentences with sleep; I whispered in Ken's bone-bare ear the responses that meant he could still be heard (though it was Marshall who changed his diapers). And from time to (too many) time I've gathered in company, ritually, to remember these and other loved men. Death's proximity. Death's daily life. As I couch myself, listening to music ["I loafe and invite my soul . . .", Whitman], I fabricate, inescapably, the tenor and texture of my own memorial. The solar-plexal moans and muscle chords of Bach's unaccompanied Cello Suites, or the harmonic inhalations of Chopin's Ballade #1, rupturing into cascades that flood the lungs as if a chest might really open into wings . . . I've attended memorials made of such deeply coded catharsis.

There's a tape you could borrow; written on its side with a blue felt pen is "Honeybear's Memorial". It contains the music Marshall assembled for his lover Ken, and the cassette box details Yoko Ono's plaintive "Beautiful Boys"; K.D. Lang wailing "So In Love"; Kiri Te Kanawa as Schubert's "Gretchen at the Spinning Wheel" (ah, *Clotho, Lachesis, Atropos*); Monserrat Caballé, from a rare live Nov. 24, 1970 recording, unveiling Bellini's aria *"Dopo l'oscuro nembo"* : "After the dark cloud", a crackling record surrounding Caballé's beneficent soprano with ambient noise, ticks, coughs, the walls themselves demonstrably reverberating and so responding; and Elisabeth Schwarzkopf ("through want and joy we have/ walked hand in hand") singing the last of Strauss's "Four Last Songs" ("At Dusk"), where the supernatural Strauss tones and planetary orchestrations disperse into even rarer constellations ("around us the valleys fold up,/ already the air grows dark") as the orbital soprano seems to unite with expanded space. Interspersed with Rilke and Whitman poems, this memorial "concert" is for Ken by Marshall, and reveals the precision of a high queen's high sentimentality, and the excess of a florid lover's furious love. *"Dass wir uns nicht verirren/ in dieser Einsamkeit"* : "We must not go astray/ in this solitude." . . . After the music we climbed Tank Hill to spread seeds of California wildflowers, as elsewhere I have tossed fistfuls of body-ash mixed with the seeds of forget-me-nots . . . We were sewing *Johnny* then, and at *his* memorial we had listened to . . .

Is it an endless threnody, then, that rehearses itself in my candle-lit house? A *melo*drama where the music *("melos")* has returned to claim the stage. Not my own valediction, but this ceremonialization proper: the power of art to encode affection itself. *The living eager attaching eros.* "Of that softest hair" (Elly Ameling sings Obradors's *"Del cabello más sutil"*) "which you wear in braids/ I must make a chain/ to draw you to my side . . ." In the music/poetic that I'm hearing, human desire is enacted in the creative strain and release of phonemes or blue notes—and these enactments, in turn, become the *objects* of desire. We adore as we listen and read; our adorations lodge. This is the charm I imagine at work cast upon Rachmaninov crescendos or Reynaldo Hahn's modulated smoke: *I* can be found there! [Whitman: "Now it is you, compact, visible, realizing my poems, seeking me . . ."]

This retrospection we might share is now engaged. A loved-one's loves are lived again in the favored words or songs that we attend. "I should like, my darling, to be a jug in your house," sings Elly as Obradors, "to kiss your lips/ when you went to drink" : *"para besarte en la boca,/ cuando fueras a besar."* Or be released as music toward your elegiac ears. Generous act of your attendance upon my own attention.

Listen: Remember me.

(1994)

Some Haunting

"He is a ghost, a shadow now, the wind by
Elsinore's rocks or what you will, the sea's
voice, a voice heard only in the heart of him
who is the substance of his shadow . . ."
—James Joyce, *Ulysses*

If he's sitting there now, it's transparently—*literally* so—
and I know he may whiff and re-congeal in another street,
another cafe. Most of the time he *(they)* will be seen from
the back, or glimpsed, peripherally, in passing; when I come
home I'll tell David, "I hallucinated Kenny today," or, "I
hallucinated John."

I'm no longer afraid these AIDS apparitions might be
real (they've lost the advantage of surprise), but my subsequent clench at the gut or failing of the knees show a
terror more truculent than fear of the Impossible. (The Impossible? What, any more, is that?) These particular visita-
tions—these "voices heard in the heart of him"—pursue.
They know my name, and my whole shaken body responds
to their address.

The ghosts who walk in my city (my ghostly city) are cast
as vividly as any childhood stored in a dipped *madeleine*—
with that fleeting precision memory affords, and the rubbed-
out edges it requires. And they rise just as suddenly. But
their appearances are oddly interdependent, communal.

They haunt *bodies* rather than places. Born as adults in affectional mutuality—exchanged caresses and comradely struggles—my reappeared friends remain so framed, and show their faces by traversing planes of living faces: faces overlaying faces. Their anxious, drifting outlines cross and merge with passing strangers—strangers filled with similar resonating passions, and hungers large enough to invite in, whole, another's presence. They flash and seize.

During these concentric crossings (I theorize) "Jackson" or "Jose" re-animate toward me, pulse for a passing moment through a flesh they once informed. Alert to the scents of shifting desires that surround them, they tremble, eyes open, through the familiar winds of social heat and social rapport. Shining eyes catch eyes; mine by their corners.

These visions are gone in the next shift of wind, of course—shift of a mouth or shoulder that reroutes the familiar image to the unfamiliar: just somebody else. Too late, for me, who have been stuck by recognition, a *madeleine*-rush of memory that comes, alas, too frequently to be savored, but whose measure is too steady to be ignored.

I am haunted.

*

Like many friends I've lost many friends to AIDS, a range of relations from intimate to "anonymous," but of them all one's incessant return puzzles me: why young John? Other friendships were dearer, others longer-lived. Yet in peripheral San Francisco his appearances, quicksilver, are inescapable: on a bicycle there in mud-green knickers, at the cafe with overstuffed art-bag slung, cruising the park with a fresh buzz cut and a goat in his gait. I haven't consciously, nostalgically looked for him; didn't *choose* to seek him out above the rest. But—rushed overlays, multiple facets of a shifting center, various frame—I'm surrounded.

It's wise Yolande explains the fact I might have known had my knees held: you *don't* choose. The ghost chooses *you!* My daily wants and needs aren't the occasion of these hauntings. Each ghost has a hunger come to me for his own fulfillment. John hungriest of all, at 28 his torn-out-of-youth death leaving live threads flailing. His compositional eye and draughtsman's hand just begun to merge common power in photography. John, whose innate interrogative restlessness allowed him to distance *and* devour, ravaging and scavenging through artforms, art histories, art communities, affinities, oppositions, to make a map his skillful unlearned feet could walk on . . . Torqued by the desperate agility of his gymnast's body he dwindled, as he grew, simultaneously, older *and* younger: an apparitional old man in padded baby diapers. John, who documented his bodily demise in a series of dispassionately precise photographs,

It's hard enough to be shamelessly naked in this body-despising culture, but to be so in a sick body when the same culture paradoxically and faddishly valorizes health takes fearlessness. That the sickness in this case is the dreaded and misunderstood AIDS makes John Davis's straightforward gaze even fiercer. Void of guilt or shame, without seeking pity: these photos do not concede. They insist on being figure studies in which a human body seeks articulation. From a leeched 97 pounds to a fluid-swollen 120, John Davis remains a figurative artist, not a disfigured one. The skeleton, the musculature, the skin and eyes: these are the working elements of a photographer /model who catches light and disposes of it formally. The courage to seek such transformations in spite of systemic pain is the heart of Davis's power. The grace of his willfulness matches it pose for pose.

—A.S., for an exhibition, 5/92

John B. Davis leaves us with an outline that is an inline: the phenomenon of his skeleton's arabesque. This unsentimental view is a gift of mortal presence, one man's self inscription, an alphabet of being. His fearlessness is awakening, and might make us each attend our own hand's particularity. AIDS brought him to this attention, in despite of its ravages. He outlasts it.

—A.S., for an exhibition, 11/93

and so fused his questions into observations *we* observe, the body's palpable inquiry extended ad infinitum.

Extended beyond those old, fixed borders, to where the gates slide easily, admitting and exiting. If he walks, as ghosts do, if he walks with me now—feeding, searching, feeding: since his very mark was *hunger* he must still be hungry! Caught fleeting and reflected in shards his raw unfinished purpose stalks the crowded streets of my city, "signalling to be opened". Haunting me it seeks completion.

How do I serve this dead young man?

(1994)

Inscribing AIDS
A Reflexive Poetics

The terror, that coming-to-get-you shark with its boom-ba boom-ba boom-ba beat, the already gotten, and the disappeared . . . or (seen from above, perhaps) the valiant, the ceaselessly experienced, the made wise, and the transcendent—all those I might truly call the authors of AIDS—for years I watched and watched myself waiting, un-verbalized, unwritten. Pressed upon, the writing task's new complexity (it might have been simplicity) bound me with awkward restless unaccustomed silence.

The idealism evident in my early poetry, which sprang from post-Stonewall enthusiasms and maintained the heady pan-social syncretic critique at large in the "underground", was already floundering under pressures from both sides: a diminishing value in gay liberation theory from the visionary to what I call—votable—the civil-libertarian, and the formal challenges agitating poetry from semiotics and linguistics. By the time, early 80s, AIDS began to claim unavoidably my most attention, the poem was emerging as explorative maneuver, and the idea of thematic writing had become problematic.

My naively confident self in whom ideologies provisionally cohered as rhetoric was cracking (or expanding), like theory's subjectivity under attack and multiple-fracturing, thousand-eyes. A poetics of inquiry and ellipsis was being privileged over one of declaration and intent. But the rupturing emergence of the epidemic ready to impale one looked monolithic from any view—hideous cyclopean frontality—and in what form could writing usefully address its brutal presence?

I saw two possible utterances relating to AIDS and its government watchdogs: Shit! and Shoot'em! The one, of loss, seemed to me woefully personal, an interjection wilder and more desperate than communication, maybe even sub-lexical; the other, of rage, was being dynamically expressed by Act Up, Queer Nation, and a host of ingenious community-indigenous organizations and I didn't see how—poetically?—to add to that.

But one may neither make meaning, as I'd thought, nor find it, after pursuit. Meaning may be delivered—bouquet or bomb—head on. For a writer, this is experienced as a demand. How to write AIDS named me.

There was no longer any way around it, only multiform ways into it. A thematic writing, then, and if so in what way, given poetry's multi focal shifting attention? I thought that "essay," narrativized as witness and textured by interrogation and digression, might hold the sought-for argument or analysis that poetry kept elliptical. A monolith is not elliptical. The pure rampage of facts unleashed by the disease demanded scrutiny, the heartbreaking lure of incessant unfolding information—to turn mortal details beneath the scoping light of sentences, to penetrate them, to release them, to be released from them. [Whitman: "As they emit themselves facts are showered over with light."]

So these nonfiction writings enmesh personal narrative and literary critical methodology, discovering that in the holistic dimension of AIDS each seemingly independent or oblique avenue leads inevitably to the viral core. Here, the procedures and vocabulary of art fuse with those of daily life—the biography of events—to demonstrate the impermissibility of such a separation under these aggressive circumstances.

I saw how theater, as dance performance with text, utilized the tensions of direct speech in a way the page couldn't, the electric tension of face-to-face confrontation and the body's tangible stresses. I wrote for dancer Ney Fonseca a piece in which the offstage voice—it may be the voice of the virus itself in its incarnation as Fate—demands that Ney encounter it—dialogic—in his own body. I'd required the dancer, HIV positive, to confront choreographically elements of his own mortality, and that encounter was the dramatic nexus of the piece. Ney was given the choice to take this on or not—he'd have to experience it each time behind a very thin screen of performance—and I knew I could merely offer him an opportunity written at the edge of propriety, threshold of permission. The risk I only wrote was one he'd have to risk.

Qualifying assent. Nonfiction writers know this scribal process better than poets who enact the Imaginative as the Real. I've passed my AIDS writings among their living sources to help determine accuracy. AIDS reality has enacted my imagination.

Poetry found its way, first as compound metaphor, then structurally. "The Depositories" and "Strips and Streamers", finding kinship in scenarios of war, estrange and re-constitute Whitman's Civil War vocabulary, pushing images of battle and comradely witness to a newly disoriented wailing point. In "Human Immune", the speaking subject inhabits experience from simultaneous locations as if all persons of voice (first, second, and third) are equally at risk. The poem proceeds formally via an epidemiological model: each "stanza" inexorably increases in length by one line, an expanding vortex. "Hell is round," the motif, revealed to me at the reservoir point after being awakened from a weeping dream-cry, may bear Dante's centripetal impasse, but also dimensionalizes AIDS from the personal to the historical: the curve one rounds is also around one, surrounding, a world. For the gay community, this circumnavigate descent can be read as the procession of history itself disappearing. *"Chi é costui che sanza morte/ va per lo regno de la morta gente?"* "Who is this that without death goes through the kingdom of the dead?"

To characterize this visceral struggle as esthetic is to rec-ognize an ecology of paradigms, a streaming mutuality of influences artistic and social, and to pay attention—poet-ics—as if one's life depended on it.

Where the relational body and the medical body use the same skin, the metaphoric implications of AIDS seem inseparable from the literal ones. A recent spontaneous mantra, passing through my regular walks in the park, announces casually, "AIDS has destroyed my life." Though presumptively antibody negative, to what extent is this a poetic figure, and who will chart the distinctions? The rising sentence has no emotional affect as it tests itself on my tongue, except the startled recognition of its effortlessly clean transmission. I blink and scour the hillside. The gnarly pines are there, and the tiny green plums, and Mt. Diablo fudged by the haze.

The matters of fact are materials. Among the interdependent life of forms characterizing human experience and the mutable various life of form we recognize as poetry, the Human Immunodeficiency Virus is also a form of life. Unchosen, unsought, it, too, inscribes a cellular plan, like the DNA code itself is said to inscribe a measure of destiny. Interactive, its dogged contentions are inescapably creative. HIV transforms, even at body's remove. The complexity of its microscopic purity rages outward. It's writing me.

(1995)

Shifting Paradise

To shewe yow the wey, in this viage,
Of thilke parfit glorious pilgrymage
That highte Jerusalem celestial
—Chaucer, *The Canterbury Tales*

I finally framed the painting by Tasha Robbins—an abstracted cross-swirl of tree stumps, raising among its energy loops a curious reminiscence of human figuration—and the portraits and posters on my old familiar walls, having duly shifted places to accommodate this newcomer, are calling to each other (to me) with reawakened vigor, as if by being moved they've fallen under new spotlights, baring their active souls again for my renewable eyes. Chairs, end-tables, moody lamps, regularly do this dance in my house, and over again what's seemed fixed loosens, reshapes interior meaning as complementary presence, pluralized out from each object or piece of art to bear relation in a cosmology of household deities.

Here on the cheap lightweight foldout bookcase—it pretends to be Japanese—under the orange volcanic vase spewing trails of eucalyptus nuts and corkscrew willows—is the one personal photo that owns a public space in my art-stuffed apartment. Five young men caught mid gambol in a park, a little chorus line of kicks, gropes, arm-over-shoulder wraps, and wide too-wide smiles. Yes, that's me (if you don't ask I'll point it out) in the wild-prophet hair and beard, a tangle of exuberant energy far the other side of saturation. My tucked-in cotton kimono's bared to the waist, where you can spot—look closely—the much-admired hand-beaded belt (snakeskin-waffled in maroon, mauve, and chalky blue) with its moon slice mother-of-pearl buckle. The ferocity of hair and pure glaze of sunlight reek of period. The year is 1975 (it's forever 1975!), the men are queer (well, one is "honorary",) and Golden Gate Park has offered its swooping cypresses and Monterey pines to border the rolling fields of that summer's Gay Freedom Day celebration.

There is no other picture, in my house, of paradise (though there is a "vale of soulmaking".) Whatever reconstellating takes place, its rarified image stays true. The spontaneous fraternal beatitude, renegade eros and radical hilarity of that San Francisco hover, like elements of celestial Jerusalem, at the apex of memory; no maturity, no fine mellowness, no deepened work dissolves them. Through the clear painterly air—as if all of San Francisco had northern light—epochal details sharpen. There, the city's edge-of-the-world history joins its urgent Pacific geography to clasp my hand in a lover's vow (I married San Francisco on a brisk craggy hilltop in 1978, in lieu of a boyfriend.) "This other-Eden, demi Paradise," rhapsodizes John of Gaunt, similarly England-besotted, "This happy breed of men, this little world,/ This precious stone set in the silver sea."

Extravagant phrases of praises gild memory—one no longer knows the actual from the iconic—the icon becomes the actual! Where physical distance blurs temporal distance refines. This much has not shifted: on a shelf a lucite frame encodes the past in a photo—unregenerate—as a paradise of pure loss.

But something has shifted: the resonant image, gingerly holding its chemical colors against the fading powers of sunlight, remains the same, but the very nature of paradise has changed. Even while—eyes dewy—focused back on primal beauty, the unforeseen—HIV—transfigures sight, beholder and beheld. "This sceptered isle," Shakespeare's Gaunt has said, "This fortress built by Nature for herself/ Against infection." The magic island is flooded in a break-away recursive tide; what did not hold—infected—returns to alter the image of origin. [Stein: "Let me recite what history teaches. History teaches."]

We stage the past in jeweled terms—to fix its daunting fluidity and give name to our nostalgia—but HIV has modified this delicate taxonomy. The paradigm shifts. A newly burnished glaze shines. A viral invasion has reconfigured the utopian body, so that what once was seen tenderly as "youth" is now revisited as the unacknowledged genius of "health".

The circling age rings in Tasha's painted tree trunks, I see today, are like the ovoid loops we practice to draw the human face. Her small oil of a foot among clouds rises, on my bedroom wall, above Nikki's green collage with its palm-

forward open hand. Familiar domestic talismans, these,—
one sleeping, the other awake—that make of any wall a window through which I view some measure of self. Catching
the last flare of sunset, they signal it across the room to a
poster, in French, for Fellini's Les Nuits de Cabiria, where
Giuletta Masina, in a chicken-feather coat, flutters her
fingers gamely at other seekers winging the night. In this
crosswind of salutations the photo from 1975 has moved to
my work table. Under gooseneck light I study its captive
luminosity: its fable of youth, to be sure, and florid sunny
conviviality, but more, now—shifted paradise—its depic-
tion, its retention, of life before AIDS.

[1995]

July

You look for summer in repeatable signs, different from pre-
ceding and subsequent days but identical to other summers,
as if in concentric loops you enter again the same zone with
the same apprehensible attributes: that dust smell of the dry
weed field by the river, the pancake of heat, or these swollen roses puffed on the dining room table, creaming pale
magenta, lavender and pink in a moire pattern, fading color
into color the way silk does, seizing light and inhabiting the
shine from within. And, too, repeatable, here at the annual
4th of July picnic, the talk has turned to weather, as over
the palomino Sonoma hills stream the first incursions of a
coming sky-wide fog.

On a low brick garden wall I pull at my turkey burger,
eyeing suspiciously the shredded carrots embedded, as Steven nudges his marinated off-the-cob corn. Last week the
heat was bone Cretan, we say, but this imminent chill at
the pool party is really the way summer seems to be head-
ing. It's OK to talk about the weather after twenty years of
casual friendship. We're all familiar here, even those of
us who don't know each other, familial, safe. We show our
aging bodies in the sun shamelessly, shorts or swim suits,
shirts or not, because at this point our physical changes,
as communal as they are inevitable, are endearing, and if
we comment we complement each other, not because we're

liars but because we appreciate—and distinguish—the difficulties. ["You are astonishing, you look as young as ever," the Duchesse de Guermantes tells Proust the narrator, and he moans to himself, "another melancholy remark, which can only mean that in fact, if not in appearance, we have grown old."] But to us even our moderate age is, we know, a rarity in plague-time; which of us will get to be old? This information passes among the passing clouds and passing sun. A barbecue is trying to nail down summer. Steven and I are laughing. Hamburger juice dribbles. From the corner of my eye I see, halfway down his calf—I hadn't known—the bright purple flower of a KS lesion.

Zalman has built a new pool; its consecration is the official business of this year's party. The pool is lovely, but the enclosure is dramatic: a white graduated stucco wall with a capping of Spanish brick hides the pool from the suburban house, and tilts the brief ascent toward Hollywood—a white terry robe could slide down your shoulders before you reach the water. In the center of the wall glass blocks turn the sunlight aqueous, and, from poolview, place us among the lapping waves of a domestic aquarium. The water is too warm, but it suits the too-threatening sky, whose heat, we see, will be short lived. A handsome man I don't know who I resisted flirting with is talking to Richard. At the end of a watery ear trumpet I hear him explaining, "The doctor wanted me to go on an IV drip just in case."

I slip-on my huaraches and stay in my wet trunks—they're new—and wander from pool to patio to kitchen, sampling the garbanzo and eggplant dips (but not the tofu) and suckling a beer. I find out the two young boys I was watching play in the water with such complete rolling body contact [Little Seryozha squirms in Anna Karenina's lap so he can touch her body to his body in as many ways as possible] that I thought, delighted, their early friendship was a paradigm of homoeroticism, are brothers and not buddies, and I wonder why their physicality now seems less sensual, as if the genetic/social sanction makes their touching unfelt. (I don't tell this to the mother.)

As usual, at parties, I'm drifting from group to grouplet, sampling conversation (but not the tofu). In the kitchen a trace scent of marijuana sparks my interest, "Do I smell something?" No answer, so I repeat it (that smell creates desire!) Marie must explain to Richard, who has the pipe, that I've asked for a hit, since I'm next to his bad ear, deaf from an AIDS infection. He lights the pipe, coming alive with his good ear, and we brighten together; the others, I believe, drift away. We drift in place.

"How are you . . .?" (The disequilibrated ear has had him dangerously ill, poisoning his bloodstream. I tell him that a ringing in my mother's ear during menopause brought her close to breakdown, though others saw it as "just a little ringing.") " . . . You seem better." He avows he is feeling better, details some doctory stuff I lose in the smoke, and adds: "I've been seeing a healer—a body and a spiritual healer— who said I should get ready for the final phase. He said to prepare for death by preparing my friends to let go of me."

For a loving man, I see, the shape of egress is correspondingly generous: he'll relinquish life by urging his loved ones to relax their hungry love that quickens him. This is posed as casual chat; the kitchen still has six desserts on the side table, the stools we sit on are these four-legged beechwood stools. Focused, we hug.

Conversational groups reform and I return to the fog-shredded light. It is not repeatable summer.

> I heard someone say that he quite looked his age, and I was astonished to observe on his face some of those signs which are indeed characteristic of men who are old. Then I understood that this was because he was in fact old and that adolescents who survive for a sufficient number of years are the material out of which life makes old men. (Proust)

Gene—a dentist and a superb chef—has cooked a glistening tart, so that the bright cherries on top are completely rounded, globular, bursting, and we joke that he must have, after baking, injected them with a dental syringe to replump them. Its perfection makes this cherry pie a sign for cherry pie. The artifice of it we recognize as drag; flour, butter, sugar, fruit in drag as a tarte aux cérises.

Fleeting disguise—the present constantly remakes itself, remasks itself, shifting. The present only stands for the present. I write this, now, on my computer, to bring to completion a book about AIDS, and it's the first piece written to be *in* the book. I've been rereading, you've noticed, part of *Remembrance of Things Past,* and it's being reread because I find I'm *in* it. I'm writing now on a log in the sun in the park and I'm back at my gray marble desk (it used to be a partition in a men's room), attempting to end a book whose original title was *Breathing Holes*—gasping up from under the ice to air— but has become, you will have read, *Unbound.*

Proust's crepuscular Baron de Charlus begins a litany:

Hannibal de Bréauté, dead! Antoine de Mouchy, dead! Charles Swann, dead! Adalbert de Montmorency, dead! Boson de Talleyrand, dead! Sosthène de Doudeauville, dead!

and my sepulchral rhymes beat instantly: Jackson Allen, dead! Charles Solomon, dead! John Davis, dead! Leland Moss, dead! as I recognize, circumnavigating, a repeatable unrepeatable necrology.

I creep into the living room to take off my still-wet trunks, almost smoked dry by the barbecue. Richard is asleep on the sofa, his long pale body soft like a child. I skinny into my green shorts quietly, not to waken him. Robert waves goodbye through the plate glass window and blows a kiss. There's some blackberry cobbler I haven't yet tried which I keep empurpled in my mind until I'm back in the kitchen eating it. Though long cooled, its deep mushy richness gives the flavor of warmth.

[1995]

Generation

The storm that raged through San Francisco late in the night of December 12, 1995 shook this whole building earthquake-style, and made a fragile raft of my bed, resting near the bay window that bucked and banged in the wind. The branches outside shrieked—I could see them whipping in the street's yellow light—and I woke and slept to repeated roaring gusts. The wind tore deep at the earth as if it wanted to get in: a thousand trees uprooted or broken in Golden Gate Park, hundreds elsewhere pulled out by their hair and lying with great clods of dirt yanked out with them, neatly serrated empty circles of shade on the ground. Gashed branches dangled everywhere; roads were blocked; the city whose trees are reaching maturity together woke to a loss that was generational: not once in a lifetime but a unified swath of lifetime lost.

My apartment could have been sliced in two by the gigantic Eucalyptus—"one of my sentinels"—across the way (a few blocks east two such aged hundred-footers crashed—into the park, as it happened, so the facing houses escaped.) But the radical size of these toppled beings was compelling; you never see them horizontally where their enormity can be measured human-scale. They were at once desperately, environmentally, evolutionarily sad, like beached whales, and gawkingly thrilling: A hundred years was lost, but the integrity with which their falling rewrote the landscape drew me to their monumental sides again and again to gape. I looked at the now-erect rootwork—multitudinous intentionality, groping—almost shamefully visible; I measured myself against the tank-like trunks which had smashed through other trees in their way, forming new tangles and bushworks of leaves, bark, and gouged-up soil. (The sound they must have made I'm glad I didn't hear.) The speed and scale of the devastation excited me even as I mourned the losses: so big I couldn't blink away the incontrovertible facts. I wanted the hugeness and the solidity of the mess, the grim external confirmation, the proud physicality literally shaken to its roots.

You can hear the metaphor forming as it forms, description snaking downwards to sink its own "ductile anchors" and prop itself up toward meaning. But I had already written, AIDS-wise: "fallen giant, empty stump" three years before these winds came wailing. In the search for accountability called mortality things expand as they contract—language, too—and "to evoke an image," as Robert Duncan says, "is to receive a sign, to bring into human language a word or a phrase of the great language in which the universe itself is written."

A fierce mutability swings us between faces of the storm.

*

In a different park—though raked by the same winds— two other fallen trees initially called me to write. A pair of massive cypresses, tenuously gripping the sandy slope in better days, have thudded down, entangling the hillside. In this park, known for its various wildness, birds relish the sudden cover: Sparrows flitter among the new-formed thickets, jays scramble, hummingbirds chortle and dive. Something fruitful has happened for them, finer and richer than any recent attempts at cultivation. For two months now I've examined the uprooted scene. Here where extravagant growth is the rule the damage seemed more easily poetic: It was comfortably, I might say conformingly, pretty. The exposed rootlets bared their fine membranes in the sun; the torn wood reddened, grass grew in the upended soil collected in the furrows of the trunks. I, too, perch here, watching the spotted hawks devour the skyline.

This little park was famously—famously!—known for casual sex, though it's been drastically pruned by AIDS, by which I mean not only that its practitioners have dwindled, but that the censors and jurists early on tried to garden away the underbrush that offered pagan cover to public acts. Though its mandated legacy to the city is untamed growth, it's managed to undergo "erosion control" in exactly those spots most lavishly used. Still, it has a flavor, and no other park foregrounds its vegetation so generously.

It has been summer in the middle of February, as sometimes happens; the air thickened, plum blossoms blew out, the sky widened. San Francisco asked to be seen. I sat on one of the fallen trunks—new branch for me!—and turned my face to the sun. The heat was saturating, liquid. I felt myself expand in the hot light, nourished.

A man I knew minimally—we never really spoke—approached and kept my eyes. I've seen him for fifteen years along a variety of erotic routes. He paused to talk about the weather—you do that in San Francisco because you like to show off your luck at living here—and eyed the tumble of branches, the inviting trouble they'd made. He thought there might be human cover there too, and chuckled at the fortuitous change. The place is ghosted—we both knew that—it was nice to contemplate a turn. "It's good to see you," he said pointedly, far more direct than either of us expected, "I mean there's so few of us left. It's good to see you still around," by which he meant "alive."

It was grass growing on top of the dying trunk that originally drew my pen, preposterous and fertile like Whitman once saw it: "And now it seems to me the beautiful uncut hair of graves.//Tenderly will I use you curling grass,/ It may be you transpire from the breasts of young men." I pushed the ruin of the storm to mean the ruin I needed. What constitutes a memorial, a legacy? Where do the bodies go I don't see go—no graves, no burning ghats—and how do they reseed a city lost to loss? (Instead of usual age-group percentages, the papers announced this week that AIDS was the leading cause of death in San Francisco, period.) I'll try to hold within my words the secrets of the sect, to reveal them in tight bouquets and thickets, in spectacular decay, a generation, a sprinkling and a rampage, I'll try to sew in you unshakably—no possible storm—the vitality whose vital signs were and are and have been palpable love.

"Then silence/ is as silence was/ again," says Robert Creeley. "That risk/ is all there is."

The famous San Francisco sun has turned to famous rain. A reminiscent wind has whipped up, strewing the gleaming street with papers and leaves, anything that rises. I imagine a series of substitutions which stand for flight: black crow, broomstick, milkweed, vapor trail, pterodactyl, red balloon, oak pollen, helicopter, luna moth, dust mote, box kite, June bug, rocket man, gazelle. The wind takes them all.

[1996]

The Dance that We Made

History has a way of reconstructing the graph of time. It binds together years, decades, centuries, epochs, and gives them names—the Stone Age, the Age of Enlightenment, the Dark Ages, the Jazz Age—solidifying the slippery past with a glaze of gravitas and grandeur. But the boundaries of these bundles remain porous and negotiable, so when Richard asked me a few years back to write the text for a dance about AIDS I hesitated, uneasy, uncertain. My memories of the epidemic were extensive and intense, but did they have—could they have *again*—the necessary power of *purpose?* Long removed from the days of terror, I needed to see if I still had a writer's projective empathy, I needed to find out exactly where I stood on the edge of the Age of AIDS.

Richard himself was returning to life as a dancer after his lover's death, after several years of his own struggle with HIV, and was making his own daily tests of flexibility and fortitude. In the '90s I'd written a book about AIDS, [this book, *Unbound*], but my immediate senses told me it had happened too long ago: I wasn't sure I could still capably represent the immediate peril and collective saturation, the daily loss and daily triumph I'd once felt (even as a "healthy" man) in *that* pandemic-era San Francisco. I was ready to surrender my impulse to collaborate, and as a kind of apologia, began a formal "letter" of explanation, a substitution, a letter dance.

*

Dear Richard,

I hallucinated you in the park today—just a guy-shadow with a similar shape—and for an instant I was able to project myself into you, enter your skin, and for an instant, I saw, possibly speak from there. It took a physical shape to seduce and activate me, where mentality and abstractions had left me wordless. A body knows from which it speaks. A body is full of information. In my thoughts I can sympathize, I can scrutinize, I can inventory and I can pray, I can ask shapely questions, suspend answers, I can even imagine myself toweling off your night sweats or carrying you up four flights of stairs if I had to. My experience resembles these actions. I can't describe your dead lover; I can't be your wounds or heal them; I can't accompany you on your well-earned victory laps. I can't be suitably astonished by the agonized body's driving force to remake itself again and again, though words resemble these experiences. I'm less than a survivor: I've just been living.

*

I'd wanted to offer Richard something in lieu of direct composition, and I knew a "story" that still wanted telling. But to write about friends dying from, surviving, or transcending AIDS, didn't I need to shoulder some burden of history, to acknowledge the frame enveloping the frame? Even now—several years after I began my letter to Richard and eight years since Marshall's death—when I'm unexpectedly seized by the untold narrative, I still wonder whether giving Marshall's death its due requires placing it *inside* the raging epidemic, San Francisco of the '80s and '90s, inside a frame of other frames, a grand, dramatic, panoramic gallery unspeakably long, or just an every- day family album stuffed with helplessly ordinary snapshots. Ah, the vital tenor, the pressure, the grief, the accuracy, the lift, the loss, the loss, the names, the language, the infancy, the phantasm, the new old age, the pure volition, the surrender, the schooling, the tender vigil, the words spoken out loud or not spoken at all or murmured into the mystery of the night, the words held in abeyance in a secret pocket for another time, another room, another improvised blessing or curse . . . But a personal request was hanging in the air; at least I might be able to offer Richard a tale to spark his dance. So in place of any newly awakened text I might muster, I continued with the letter.

*

My dead friend Marshall wants me to tell you part of his story, which I observed, and which I have remembered. His final frailty was thorough and precise, a total deconstruction, so complete it remained out of reach of sentimental projection or exaggerated sympathy. His wasted body small to begin with dwindled inward to a point, a disappearing act, a fact. His ears gone deaf three months previously, his eyes shut down to light and shade: a secret man. That might have been his story if you hadn't known the people we've known.

He'd been raving semi-coherently about a lovely man who'd been delivered to him by a friend—the last newcomer to be actually seen (though Marshall had barely known him, and he'd already departed weeks ago)— and who'd become, *since* then, blind Marshall's spirit guide, his angel of death (I thought) to whom he spoke lovingly and reverently as an eternal beloved— pure intimate address—when others were gathered around, and often when they weren't. "Arno," who even in absence kept Marshall's vocabulary elevated with thrilling, seat-of-the- pants passion and courtly, troubadour vows. "*Arno,*" whose lyrical name and recollected visage Marshall then placed on anyone else in actual attendance, speaking with fervent, conspiratorial fixation, *"There you are."* We were all guises of this one demon lover, whose skin and face slipped over each of us like a sheath, and whose interactive, high-minded ardor we duly impersonated. We didn't correct Marshall, since in our friendships we resembled this devotion. We were all of us willingly *Arno*. A convention of Great Beloveds assembled in his room or near his bed, and we each entered the cottage zone prepared for this hushed intensity, the last cleared circle of theatrical redemption: love in bloom.

*

I put my letter to Richard aside for a while. A story is not a dance, I knew, but I had in my hands only what I had in my head. Stories, I know, circle even when they aren't told (the letter was written but wasn't sent) so that even now, years later, I'm driven, again, to tell. On *this* day in April after relentless, record-breaking rains, the sun—hello, stranger— has yanked up the first alarming crop of wildflowers, and the word "bouquet" is fresh on my tongue from yesterday's email (I'd petulantly told a recalcitrant potential date that I had "collected my little bouquet of 'no's'" and would wait for *him* to contact *me!*). In this floral melodrama, Marshall inescapably sits on my shoulder once more, and I return to a letter never sent and never really completed to finish a narrative looking for continuity.

*

Zalman, Marshall's main caregiver, had given over his bungalow to Marshall's final months, his final days, his breath or two, this winnowing fade. Through the Petaluma summer's long heat, Marshall had tended a small backyard garden, prize endeavor and joyous, creative tether. By August his eyes were gone, but the garden was bright in his heart and he was kept apprised of its progress. Now, at last—September's flourish—the plot was in high bloom. From the blind bed on which his bones floated, Marshall asked Zalman, one of the only friends whose personal touch he actually recognized (one of the few who weren't "Arno"), in a voice part solicitous and part rich with command, "Bring me some flowers, please."

Zalman went to the back of the house and cut a fine bouquet—flowers resemble our best intentions—then happily brought an overflowing vase to Marshall in bed: buoyant zinnias in transcendental hues, pledge and proof of summer's forward-looking zeal. He guided Marshall's bony hands to feel the curl and bend and flute of each open corolla. With delicate care Marshall sculpted in air, lightly caressing petal and crown, molding the blossoms into a proud, pantomime bouquet. He leaned forward to inhale, where hearing and sight were beyond him, to bring into his body this fist of full bloom. A small shudder rolled across his face. Slowly, carefully, Marshall grasped the brimming vase in both hands and thrust it across the wide bed directly toward Zalman. Then with arms outstretched and filled with flowers, he whispered excitedly, "They're for *you!*"

*

Dear Richard, this is my dance for you, insofar as it resembles the movement you can make of it. I've seen such things!—some of which I can tell, in the small ways in which I'm the semblance of the friends I've known. This world, in the end, "corresponds to itself," of which we partake with gusto.

*

The tentative letter remained uncompleted inside of my computer. In the end, I flew from San Francisco to New York in order to watch Richard dance in his studio, to see if his living, gesturing body could awaken in mine the necessary memory of the necessary urgency of AIDS— cast now as the measure of *his* endurance. In a rickety downtown studio, on a folding chair in the filtered light, I felt Richard's muscles pull against their limits, then trembled with the challenge each extension and propulsion made visible. Within minutes his movement *remembered* me, made me actively engaged in a long struggle familiar, estranged, but retained in my body the way steps imprint themselves in a dancer's corporal recall. I proceeded, then, to collaborate with Richard on a new solo for him, while Paula composed a score: text, movement, music in alliance, a model of walking, looking, and thinking. In the piece, Richard's slow-motion weave through space is a paced enactment of composure and focus. Against gravity, amidst the hurrying furies, he has surrendered to the fixity of his own deliberate gaze.

Here is the opening of the dance that we made:

*

Sky panels move and shift. Things move *through* them and *in* them. Clouds, birds, airplanes; the spires of tall buildings. The sky moves *in* me and *through* me. Air currents swirl and bend; my back bends forward in the wind. On the pavement in a gray puddle the sky shimmers bluely, a pinch of white dissolving as the cloud-wisps drift.

Sky panels scroll and shift. The fat, feathery clouds are bunched with gray bottoms, white contours. A sea-blue hole like an eye watches a gull swoop. It moves *under* the sky, not *in* it. A corniced building cuts into the edge of a cloud mass, where a darker gray comprises the heart of the cloud. It moves *in* me, not *over* me.

Sky panels widen. A gleam of sunlight pulls at the feathers of the clouds, spreading them but also spreading the gray—which turns darker, thicker, as if a fuzz were on it. Patterns of shadow cut and lace the pavement, moving *over* it and *on* it. The red in the brick wall pulsates, then fades.

Sky panels shuffle and tense. White serrates the middle of a cloud bank, then rips. It tears *through* me and past me. Car hoods shine metallic under the glare, almost wet with light. A seam of blue widens then closes, sutured. A small hole stays visible, and light rushes into it. It folds shut, but lip edges are flushed with white. They're absorbed inward and move off. Two pigeons punctuate the rooftop in silhouette, featureless but ruffled against the shifting gray.

A panel of sky unmoving. It holds me and I hold it. Layers and layers of petaled gray, deeper and deeper towards a whitish core, where a wash of light hangs suspended. The interior panels congeal and separate, but the outer frame remains whole, fixed. It sucks *in* and blows *out*. A taxi idles, pulling the sky into its windshield where no passenger sits, as if a streak or a flash were frozen.

Sky panels shift and move. Bright masses push gray masses out of the way, making the out-spread wings of the pigeons transparent. A flare of sunlight catches the rooftop, turning the granite metallic. Something like heat falls from the sky, passing *through* me. A gray mass nudges past the white. A woman's hair stands perpendicular in the breeze, pointing toward the sky, which coalesces around a dark spot then disperses. An island of blue is glimpsed *inside* the clouds; it's *behind* them and *through* them; they move *over* it and *on* it, but they don't move past it. The nearest cloud seems to silver the whole street. I move *in* it and *on* it as the sky moves through.

(2003)

EPILOGUE

Binding *Unbound*
An Introduction to *Unbound: A Book of AIDS*

Preface from *The Skin of Meaning:*
Collected Literary Essays and Talks, 2016

Among the literary texts and talks collected here that arose alongside my poetry in a heady period of theory and critique—flowering in particular after my studies in poetics at New College of California—*Unbound* is at the heart of the matter. The penetrating sorrow of AIDS, the shock, the depth-charge, the limitlessness ("unbound"), the arc of inquiry, the angels, the call to order, the call to death, the call to life: all these passions of the epidemic pulled at my essay writing as of some primal eros or anti-eros. They demanded the figure of a mortal body to house their contending forces. As the human body was the form in which the meaning of the virus found agency, so my writing about the epidemic would shape itself towards bodies as a formal principle. In other words, the analysis—the *poetic* analysis—would be channeled through people in time and space—in *history*—and the essays in *Unbound* would structure themselves as a new (to me) kind of poetic *narrative,* where revelations were attached to actual names, and the viral ink documented its transit in the stories and speeches of my friends who were its actual hosts.

My poetry had already engaged the form of the prose-poem

to unwind mini-narratives, queered by radical ellipsis and mysteriously free-floating subjectivity, but *Unbound*, with its urgent figures and voices, led me toward a critical writing also housed in narrative. I'd previously committed myself to the first-person voice in both prose and poetry, as a means of destabilizing authority and undermining the fiction of objectivity. No high-floating blind statements of supposed facts, or pseudo-neutral, "One could say that . . ." Bent along the informing angles of gender, queerness, and identity formation, the speaking subject with a house of skin and bones would be my petitioner. Mine was not going be a disembodied poetics! But with its information inextricably linked to the lives of my friends, AIDS raised the stakes to make neutrality impossible and subjectivity *comprehensive.*

And yet, as much as "body" absorbed "theory" into its membranes, theory demanded that body also be symbolic, polymorphous, historicized, and self-analytical (or should I say self-diagnostic?) Skin would be informed by meaning, and meaning by skin. From the beginning the essays in *Unbound* were viewed as part of my work in poetics, exactly as the guiding impulse at the root of my inquest was a search through the bones of the epidemic for poetic meaning. I wanted information subtler than statistics, deeper than diagnosis, more pitched than mourning, rawer than memory and richer than fact, grander than benedictions . . . ignited by a mortal fire but outlasting it. I wanted to wrest a poem's meaning from the epidemic's prose—the quotidian facts, the journalism, the indexed obituaries. And I wanted to use prose to dissect the epidemic, and lay bare its poetic heart: the quoted language of transcendence, the angelic clarity and sorrowful wisdom. Almost to the end, in fact, *Unbound*'s subtitle was, "A Poetics of AIDS." (Its actual working title was a resonant but unfortunate phrase taken from one of the essays: *Mortal Purposes.* Alas I kept saying to myself, *"Myrtle Porpoises,"* and had to send both purpose and porpoise back to the blue wild . . .) *Unbound* took shape in the grip of personal narrative—balancing daily fact and daily awe—and the flare of poetic attention—fusing the familiar and the extraordinary.

The circumstances were overripe with emotion, and easily overwhelming, and I didn't have scientific distance—medical or social. Poetics also meant the angle *in.* I had in mind a passage from Claude Lanzmann's holocaust documentary *Shoah,* in which Polish townsfolk accept culpability for a particularly brutal and efficient extermination process because Lanzmann asks them questions of such specificity that they get lost in the details and forget the larger guilt—details, for example, about the carpentry and measurements of what is essentially an execution platform. AIDS cut such a wide and jagged swath across our lives (I want to say its scythe did) that I sought to enter at an angle or an edge, often arriving on the associative vibrations of literature and art: the reverberations of a pictorial image or a quoted line. *Unbound* is replete with citations from my contributing heroes Shakespeare, Chaucer, Whitman, Proust, Stein and

Cocteau; with evocations of the music of Chopin and Verdi, of the golden throats of Monserratt Caballe and Aprile Millo, or the violet eyes of Elizabeth Taylor; with examinations of photographs in single and in sequence, and articulations of the dancer *and* the dance. The pieces partook of my life in letters and art because they partook of my life in letters and art. The impulse was holistic. The subtitle ultimately became "A Book of AIDS" much as if it had been a day book or a book of hours, where AIDS was equal to the day or the hour.

Almost all of the writing in *Unbound* appeared in the same journals and presses that were publishing my poetry. I was aggressively determined that this writing be seen as central to my literary work; I was uniformly insistent that I lacked the luxury to frame another discourse; and I was achingly aware that those not inside the circle of fire had very little idea of the intensity and the enormity of the flames. And so *Unbound* was published in book form by the fine literary press, Sun & Moon, which had already published my poetry collection *Into Distances*. The essays appeared in *Poetics Journal, Talisman, Temblor* and *ACTS*. I should say with respect that though I came armed for battle, the editors of these publications met me with high interest and regard. Nevertheless, there was very little other writing related to AIDS appearing in these journals, and if I sometimes felt ferociously isolated, the isolated circumstances fueled my ferocity. I had already published and read a fair amount of homo-centric work in the same or similar venues, behind an imaginary "I know what I'm talking about so shut up and listen" guard, and I used to joke admiringly that the largely hetero audiences actually did. In truth, many of the barriers I blew down were internal, but in any event they were downed.

Unbound formed in the clearing as a series of inquiries and interjections, a rising arc inside a descending spiral, a way out that was a way in. And if I have given the impression that my endeavors were somehow heroic, it is a fiction of the shorthand of my telling. I agonized over how to write; I was late to the task; I trembled nervously over the transcendental gifts my friends had given me. But I was surrounded by what I might properly call a sense of duty, even if it at times it felt like nowhere to run: AIDS chased me down, cornered me, and stuck a pen in my hand.

(2016)

Preface to *Unbound: A Book of AIDS*

Original preface, Sun & Moon Press, 1997

Around 1982 a young man I knew opened up his mouth and showed me the deep inside of his upper palate where a few pale areas represented Kaposi's sarcoma. His mouth was dark—ah, sweet vulnerability!—and I could barely detect (we were at work, no flashlight) the differences in shading he spoke of. That fearful subtlety was so telling his mouth—dark oracle—remains open before me: I'm still listening to what it has to say.

I'm still writing into what it has to say. The *range* of information AIDS presents keeps one at full attention. Who knew, to begin, what dimensions the replicate virus would come to occupy? The various works collected here are the stations of an enlarging question: the question, alarmed, of a cell aroused by invasion, or the yearning curl of a lover's body awake on the vacated sheets.

There was no project; I've been learning to write about AIDS piece by piece *through* piece by piece. I've dated the texts here, and let facts and figures remain as they were originally, to mark the developing way. But the numbers, their aggregate lines, (their additions, multiplications and subtractions), were not my story. For that reason I call this small but incremental book a poetics: Its way was made with both hands stretched, investigative, crossing and recrossing.

The process—poetic, even lyric—tests the threads as it leads them—as it's led by them—and coaxes their meeting, otherwise statistical, toward meaning(s).

Reading backward I seem, now, to have started each piece from ground zero, trying to capture the whole of AIDS in a swipe, from an unanticipated slant. Each time, it seems, some face of mortality was there to surprise me, with its furious broadside view too spacious for my narrow-set eyes, sky-wide and roiling and only just for the moment separate, avoidable. My own ever-baby face receded, as I stood in the shadows and watched the light flame others. The writing progressed as narration.

Authority?—*not* mine, but an urge toward the integration of fear and immutable fact, and a heart for consequence. Who could have moved me to this end but the men whose names are mentioned here, who were my informants and guides, and whose natural affectional alliances made an epidemic based on love and desire possible? It soon became clear that for me writing about AIDS was weighted toward witness. Such participation's cursèd rare privilege is offered to you.

(1997)

NOTES

Jean Cocteau, *Orphée [Orpheus]*, André Paulvé and Les Films du Palais-Royal, 1950

Robert Creeley, ["Then silence/ is as silence was,"] "Waiting," *Words,* Charles Scribner's Sons, 1967

H.D., "The Walls Do Not Fall," *Trilogy,* New Directions, 1973

Richard Daniels, dancer/choreographer, and Paula Kimper, musical composer, "Sky Panels" from *Bonus Round,* ["The Dance that We Made,"] first performed April 2, 2003, at the Connelly Theater, New York City

Dante [*"Chi é costui che sanza morte,"*] *Inferno,* Canto VIII

Robert Duncan ["Our uses are our illuminations,"] *The H.D. Book,* edited by Michael Boughn and Victor Coleman, University of California Press, 2011

D. H. Lawrence ["Why does the thin grey strand,"] "Sorrow," *Selected Poems,* The Viking Press, 1961

Claude Lanzmann, *Shoah,* BBC and others, 1985

Fernando Obradors, "del cabello más sutil," Elly Ameling, *Serenata,* Phillips

Marcel Proust, *A Remembrance of Things Past,* trans. C.K. Scott Moncrieff, Vintage Books, 1982

William Shakespeare ["This sceptred isle,"] *Richard II,* Act 2, Scene 1

Aaron Shurin, "City of Men," *A's Dream,* O Books, 1989

Aaron Shurin, "Turn Around" with Ney Fonseca, first performed for Juntos Dance, Theatre Artaud, San Francisco, October 1992

Gertrude Stein ["Let me recite what history teaches,"] "If I Told Him:

101

A Completed Portrait of Picasso," *Look at Me Now and Here I Am,* Penguin Books, 1971

Richard Strauss, "Four Last Songs," Elizabeth Schwarzkopf, George Szell conductor, EMI Classics

Giuseppe Verdi, *Aida,* Act IV, Scene 2, Metropolitan Opera Orchestra and Chorus, Sony Classical

Walt Whitman, ["The Depositories," "Strips and Streamers"] "Specimen Days", *Prose Works, 1892,* New York University Press, 1963 and *Leaves of Grass, Comprehensive Reader's Edition,* W.W. Norton & Co., 1965

ACKNOWLEDGMENTS

Grateful acknowledgement is given to Sun & Moon press, the original publishers of *Unbound: A Book of AIDS* (1997), and to editor/publisher Douglas Messerli for his consummate support of the work. Gratitude as well to the University of Michigan press, for permission to reprint from *The Skin of Meaning: Collected Literary Essays and Talks* (2016), and to City Lights for "The Dance that We Made" from *King of Shadows* (2008), reprinted with the permission of The Permissions Company, LLC, on behalf of City Lights Books.

A special thanks goes to the extraordinary crew steering the Nightboat, steady as she goes, full speed ahead. And to Stephen Motika and Kazim Ali, for their tireless pursuit of the marvels of the art.

for

Jackson Allen (1945–1987)

Ken Andreotta (1956–1991)

John B. Davis (1964–1992)

Eric Moore (1949–1984)

Leland Moss (1949–1990)

Marshall Rheiner (1951–1998)

Chuck Solomon (1946–1986)

AARON SHURIN is the author of fourteen books of poetry and prose, most recently *The Blue Absolute* (Nightboat, 2020), *Flowers & Sky: Two Talks* (2017), and *The Skin of Meaning: Collected Literary Essays and Talks* (2015). His work has appeared in over forty national and international anthologies, from *The Norton Anthology of Postmodern American Poetry* to *Italy's Nuova Poesia Americana: San Francisco*, and has been supported by grants from The National Endowment for the Arts, The California Arts Council, The San Francisco Arts Commission, and the Gerbode Foundation. A pioneer in both LGBTQ studies and innovative verse, Shurin was a member of the original Good Gay Poets collective in Boston, and later the first graduate of the storied Poetics Program at New College of California. He has written numerous critical essays about poetic theory and compositional practice, as well as personal narratives on sexual identity, gender fluidity, and the AIDS epidemic. A longtime educator, he's the former director and currently Professor Emeritus for the MFA Writing Program at the University of San Francisco.

NIGHTBOAT BOOKS

Nightboat Books, a nonprofit organization, seeks to develop audiences for writers whose work resists convention and transcends boundaries. We publish books rich with poignancy, intelligence, and risk. Please visit nightboat.org to learn about our titles and how you can support our future publications.

The following individuals have supported the publication of this book. We thank them for their generosity and commitment to the mission of Nightboat Books:

Anonymous (4)
Kazim Ali
Abraham Avnisan
Jean C. Ballantyne
The Robert C. Brooks Revocable Trust
Amanda Greenberger
Rachel Lithgow
Anne Marie Macari
Elizabeth Madans
Elizabeth Motika
Thomas Shardlow
Benjamin Taylor
Jerrie Whitfield & Richard Motika

This book is made possible, in part, by grants from the New York City Department of Cultural Affairs in partnership with the City Council, the New York State Council on the Arts Literature Program, and the Topanga Fund, which is dedicated to promoting the arts and literature of California.